CATALOGUE OF THE

GREEK COINS OF

CRETE AND THE AEGEAN ISLANDS.

BY

WARWICK WROTH.

EDITED BY

REGINALD STUART POOLE, LL.D.

CORRESPONDENT OF THE INSTITUTE OF FRANCE.

1886.

EDITOR'S PREFACE.

THIS volume of the Catalogue of Greek Coins in the British Museum contains the money of Crete and of the Islands of the Aegean to which the ancient Geographers applied the names of Cyclades and Sporades.

The metal of each coin is stated, and its size in inches and tenths, and the weight of the gold and silver coins is given in English grains. Tables for converting grains into grammes and inches into millimètres, as well as into the measures of Mionnet's scale, are placed at the end of the volume.

The work has been written by Mr. Warwick Wroth, of the Department of Coins; and I have carefully revised it, comparing every coin with the corresponding description.

REGINALD STUART POOLE.

CONTENTS.

§ 2. Aegean Islands—

CRETE :—

INDEXES :—

INTRODUCTION.

CRETE.

Ancient and modern sources of information.

MOST of the ancient sources of information respecting the island of Crete were first collected in the learned work of Meursius—*Creta Cyprus Rhodus*, published at Amsterdam in 1675. In the early part of the present century appeared the well-known *Kreta* of Hoeck,* an erudite book, but one which somewhat errs on the side of over-elaborateness. MM. Bolanachi and Fazy have given a readable summary of it in their *Précis de l'Histoire de Crète.*† Several modern travellers, particularly Pashley,‡ Spratt,§ and Thénon,‖ have also added to our knowledge of the island, and have rendered good service by identifying ancient sites. Bursian, in his *Geographie von Griechenland* (vol. ii. pp. 529—581), has given a useful account of the various Cretan cities, and has incorporated much of the material which has accumulated since the time of Hoeck.¶ Our

* Göttingen, 1828 (3 vols.).

† Paris, 1869; Part ii. of the work deals with the post-classical history of Crete, on which see also G. Perrot's *L'île de Crète*, Paris, 1867.

‡ Pashley, *Travels in Crete*, 2 vols., Cambridge and London, 1837.

§ Captain [now Admiral] Spratt, *Travels and Researches in Crete*, 2 vols., London, 1867.

‖ Thénon in *Revue archéologique*, N.S., vols. xiv.—xviii.

¶ Cf. also Schömann, *Griechische Alterthümer*, p. 295 ff. (Eng. trans., 1871); Hermann, *Lehrbuch der griech. Staatsalterth.* (1875), §§ 21, 22, and Caillemer's art. *Cretensium Respublica* in Daremberg and Saglio, *Dict. des Ant.*

b

archaeological sources of information, if we except the coins and various lapidary inscriptions, must be pronounced to be but meagre, Crete never having been systematically excavated.

Cretan History.

The incidents of Cretan history* are of a somewhat uninteresting and even ignoble character. If we would seek the true glories of Crete we must turn to her legendary foretime, to the days of Minos and of Daedalus; to the days when Agamemnon, King of men, rejoiced before Troy as he saw the Cretans arming around the warlike Idomeneus: for they all "were skilled in warring, neither did disheartening dread keep back a man of them, nor did any one, yielding to coward sloth, avoid the evil contest." To the not unwholesome, but almost too thoroughgoing scepticism of the historian Grote, the legends of Minos and the rest remained mere legends; they were as curtains which might, indeed, conceal behind them figures of flesh and blood, but curtains which could not by any possibility be withdrawn. According to the more brilliant, and probably more discerning criticism of Curtius (*Hist. of Greece*, i., p. 71 f., English translation), there attaches to the Crete of Minos the notion of a marked historical epoch of civilization. Minos himself may be looked upon as the first sea-king, the Lord of the Isles of Hellas. It is true (says Curtius) that the nebulous veil of myth will hardly enable us to recognize the outlines of historical personages, but yet it is not difficult to make out that the essence of the legends of Minos consists in the fact that "order and law, the foundation of states, and a variety of forms of divine worship, originated in his island." Open to three continents at once—to Greece, to Libya, and to Asia—and especially to the

* This sketch of Cretan history and certain other portions of the Introduction are reproduced with some modifications from the essay on 'Cretan Coins' published by the present writer in the *Numismatic Chronicle* for 1884, vol. iv., 3rd series, pp. 1—58.

civilising influences of Phrygia and Phoenicia, Crete gave birth to a civilization which bore a Hellenic stamp, and which was formed "out of the confused minglings of different phases of nationality by a process of elimination and refinement." The recovery of the historic element in legend is obviously a difficult if not exactly an impossible task, but there can be little doubt that well-directed excavations might discover in Crete, as they have at Mycenae and elsewhere, a clue to many dubious points in its early history, and even perhaps afford their solution. What, for instance, was the precise extent of that Phrygian and Phoenician influence in Crete which we now but dimly apprehend, mainly through the obscure indications of certain myths? What is the true significance of legends like those of Daedalus? Does the Egyptian information as to the maritime races of the Mediterranean, B.C. 1500-1200, illustrate the Thalassocracy of Minos? Was Crete, as Dr. Milchhoefer (*Die Anf. d. Kunst*) has maintained, an important centre of primitive artistic energy? These are questions which it might be possible for archaeology to answer, and upon which even the acutest literary criticism cannot claim to have said the last word.

But it is not so much with the half-mythical past of Crete, as with its recorded history that the numismatist is concerned. And first, we must notice how largely the whole course of Cretan history was determined by the geographical conformation of the island itself. Broken up into valleys, divided one from another by barriers of mountain, Crete seemed to present a physical obstacle to political union and centralization. Though certain traits of character and forms of polity, though the worship of certain divinities, as of the goddess Britomartis, or Diktynna, are found throughout the island, the history of Crete is principally the history of individual Cretan cities, each with its own government and isolated interests; each striking its own coins, and even using its own especial calendar.

The history of these cities in their earlier days is very imperfectly known to us: we know, however, that the various streams of Cretan activity never mingled with the broad sea of Hellenic life. From the glorious contest with the Persians Crete stands aloof; she has neither part nor lot in the great inter-Hellenic war of the fifth century.* The Cretans are always too much pre-occupied with their own internal struggles, and if they are found fighting beyond the limits of their island it is in the character of mercenaries, embracing any cause for pay. Three of the Cretan cities, namely Cnossus, Gortyna, and Cydonia, seem to tower above the rest, but we find them now united, now disunited, just as it suits their temporary purpose. Of these and of the other cities we obtain more frequent glimpses as time advances. A number of inscriptions belonging chiefly to the end of the third century B.C., record the treaties made between various communities of Crete—the alliance of Latus with Olus, of Hierapytna with Priansus, of Hierapytna with Lyttus, of Dreros, Cnossus and Miletus against Lyttus;† and these inscriptions, together with the details given by Polybius, enable us to form some general notion of Cretan politics, and of the vehement strife of city with city. In B.C. 216 we find the Cretans, weary for a time of their internecine struggles, inviting Philip V. of Macedon to assume the general protection of the island; but no pressure from without seems ever to have much affected the petty course of Cretan history, or to have forced the cities into a really permanent union. In the second and first centuries before our era, the Cretans came into contact with the power of Rome, and in B.C. 67 the island,

* Thuc. vii. 57 seems an exceptional instance.

† See a list in Hicks, *Manual of Grk. Inscripts.* p. 295; cf. also *Bull. de Corr. hell.* iii. (1870), p. 290 f.; Cauer, *Delectus* (2nd ed.), p. 70; Lebas-Waddington, iii., p. 28 ff. On the important legal inscription of Gortyna, discovered in 1884 by Halbherr and Fabricius, see the monographs of Baunack, Bücheler, Comparetti, Lewy, &c.; and cf. Merriam in *American Journal of Archaeology*, 1885.

which had long been a stronghold of pirates, was finally reduced (not without some display of native bravery) by the Roman general Metellus, who thus acquired his surname Creticus.

Of the numerous cities of Crete more than thirty are known to have issued coins. In addition to the cities represented in the British Museum Collection, Biennus, Ceraeae, Lisus, Tanus (Imhoof-Blumer, *Monnaies grecques*, p. 220), and, according to Von Sallet (*Zeit. f. Num.*, xii. (1885), pp. 359, 360), Matalon (or Matalia), also coined money.

Coin-issuing cities

The arrangement of the coins in chronological order is not an easy task, and is, as a rule, but little facilitated by such knowledge as we possess of the history of the cities individually, and of their relations with one another. The evidence of *style*, moreover, usually so valuable to the numismatist, is here, to a great extent, unavailable, on account of the peculiar and frequently barbarous character of Cretan coin-art. The chronological sequence of the coins would, in fact, be far more uncertain than it is, were it not that the inhabitants of Crete had an especial fondness for using the coins of other Greek peoples as *flans* upon which to impress their own devices and legends. Dr. Friedlaender, in an article in the *Zeitschrift für Numismatik* (iv. p. 337 f.), has called attention to some of these restrikings, and others will be found in this Catalogue. These restruck pieces, when they can be identified and dated, as is the case with the coins of Cyrene, which served as *flans* for the Gortynian money, enable us to establish one or two tolerably fixed points in Cretan coinage.*

Chronological arrangement of the Coins.

* Metrological considerations are not of much importance in arranging the bulk of Cretan money, though at a late period, apparently about the end of the third century B.C., coins of reduced Attic weight begin to take the place of the earlier coins which are based on the Aeginetic and Persian standards.

The majority of the coins may be approximately assigned to the following six periods :—

I. *circ.* B.C. 500—431.
II. „ „ 431—300.
III. „ „ 300—200.
IV. „ „ 200—67.
V. „ „ 67—27.
VI. Imperial Coinage.

The numismatic annals of Crete are nearly barren during the earlier part of the fifth century, and the first issue of money in most of the cities takes place within the limits of our second period. The earliest coins in the present period seem to belong to about the beginning of the fifth century, while the latest were probably issued more than thirty years or so before the close of that century. The exact date, B.C. 431, as the downward limit of our first, and the upward limit of our second period, has been selected as one easily remembered from its being also the date of the outbreak of the Peloponnesian War: so far as we know, however, that war had no direct influence on Cretan politics or Cretan coinage. Only some five or six of the 'hundred cities' of Crete are at present known to have issued coins during the period now under discussion. As might be expected, the important cities of Cnossus and Gortyna are in possession of coinages of considerable extent before B.C. 431: it is curious, however, that no early money of Cydonia should be forthcoming. It is also doubtful whether we have any very early coins of Lyttus, though Lyttus is one of the Cretan localities mentioned in Homer. Phaestus, likewise mentioned in the Homeric Poems, was, on the other hand, certainly one of the first towns in Crete to issue money, as is proved by the existence of the unique didrachm in the British Museum, described on page 61, no. 1, pl. xiv. no. 14 (cf. Wroth,

Period I. circ. B.C. 500—431.

Cretan Coins, p. 45). This coin bears in every respect a very close resemblance to a well-known didrachm of Gortyna, formerly in the Collection of General Fox (see Fox, *Engravings of unedited or rare Greek Coins*, pt. i. pl. x., no. 109; cf. *Revue Num.*, 1864, p. 103 f.), and now in the Berlin Museum. The inscriptions *Φαιστίων τὸ παῖμα* and *Γορτύνος τὸ παῖμα* are very remarkable, and the specimens on which they occur are doubtless the earliest inscribed, if not the earliest issued, coins of Crete. The archaic forms of the letters, especially the forms of sigma, iota and mu, and the form **C** for **Π** and also for **Φ** are interesting, and should be compared with those of the early lapidary inscriptions of Cretan *provenance*. (See Thénon in *Revue arch.*, vol. viii. N. S. p. 444; Bréal, *Rev. arch.*, vol. xxxvi. N. S. p. 346 f.; *Mittheilungen d. deutschen arch. Institutes in Athen*, vol. ix. (1884), p. 363 ff; *Bull. de corr. hell.*, vol. ix. (1885), pp. 1—6). These two coins of Gortyna and Phaestus, besides being similar in the form of their legend are also similar in type (*obv.* Europa on bull, *rev.* Lion's head). What precise political or religious relations between the two cities are pointed to by this similarity of legend and type, it is difficult to say. Europa is the natural type of Gortyna, but the lion's head, though it occurs on several early coins of that city, has, so far as can be ascertained, no such close connection with Gortynian cultus and myth. It is possible that the lion's head may be really the property of the Phaestians, for whom, as a symbol of their divinity Herakles, it would be appropriate. In addition to Cnossus, Gortyna, and Phaestus, the town of Praesus (the earliest historical mention of which occurs in Herodotus vii. 170, 171) issued coins during this period: they are not however of such high antiquity as the earliest specimens of the three cities just referred to. Some of the earliest coins of Itanus, and the earliest inscribed pieces of Lyttus, probably also belong to our first period, though to the later rather than to the earlier part of it.

Most of the coin-issuing Cretan cities struck money during the second period. These coinages include some of the finest specimens in point of art, as well as other specimens which are characteristically Cretan both in their choice of types and in the barbarous or quasi-barbarous character of their work. The great cities of Cnossus and Gortyna continue to issue coins abundantly, and Cydonia now first appears with money dating from the beginning of the fourth century B.C. Itanus, Lyttus, Phaestus and Praesus also continue their coinages. Besides Cydonia, the following cities have a coinage of their own for the first time—Aptera, Axus, Chersonesus, Eleuthernae, Hierapytna,* Naxos, Phalasarna, Polyrhenium, Priansus, Rhaucus, Sybrita and Tylisus.

Period II. circ. B.C. 431—300.

The coins belonging to the third period seem to be comparatively few. It is possible, though there is apparently no evidence from Finds, that the coins of Alexander circulated in the island, and eked out the scanty native currencies. L. Müller (*Numismatique d'Alexandre le Grand*, pp. 227—231, nos. 900—909) has assigned Alexandrine coins to five cities—Lyttus, Itanus, Aptera, Cydonia, Phalasarna, but the attribution of these pieces cannot be regarded as certain. The alliances contracted by the various Cretan cities with one another during the third century B.C., of which we know the details from inscriptions (see above, p. xii), do not generally seem to have left their traces on the coinage, though of one remarkable alliance certain coins of Cnossus (p. 22 nos. 35—39; pl. vi. nos. 1, 2, 3) furnish, as can hardly be doubted, an interesting numismatic record. These coins show conjoined on the same specimen the types distinctive of Cnossus and of Gortyna—namely, the Labyrinth and Europa seated

Period III. circ. B.C. 300—200.

* For the remarkable coin of Hierapytna (*circ.* B.C. 400) with *Lycian* types, see Imhoof-Blumer in *Zeit. f. Num.*, vol. xiii. pl. iv. no. 8.

on the bull;* and this combination can surely only point to some actual alliance between these two rival cities. It is recorded by Polybius (iv. 53—55; cp. vii. 12, 9) that in the year 220 B.C. a league was constituted between Cnossus and Gortyna, the object of which was to bring the other cities of Crete under their supreme control; and in this object, we are told, they succeeded, though the important town of Lyttus at first held out against them. That Cnossus should on this occasion give an additional emphasis to the alliance by admitting the coin-types of her great ally to a place on her own coinage is not at all unlikely, and on grounds of style also the coins may well be assigned to the end of the third century B.C.

The coin of Polyrhenium on pl. xvii., no. 1, may also possibly be connected with a historical event. The head on the obverse is considered by Prof. Percy Gardner (*Types*, pl. xii., p. 204) and by the author of the *Guide to the Coins of the Ancients* (pl. 32, 26; cf. Mionnet, ii. p. 293, no. 280; Wroth, *Cretan Coins*, p. 53), who have previously published the coin, to be an Apollo, though, as the former points out, it is obviously the head of some human personage in the character of that god. Mr. Gardner is rather inclined to think that the personage here represented is Perseus, king of Macedon, though the head does not bear a very close likeness either to Perseus or to Philip V. of Macedon, another possible claimant. Of the two, perhaps Philip is to be preferred, for we know that about B.C. 220 (a not improbable date for the coin on stylistic and metrological grounds) he had relations with the people of Polyrhenium. In that year the Polyrhenians united themselves with other Cretan cities to succour Lyttus, which was then attached by Cnossus. Lyttus was destroyed, but the Polyrhenians and their allies continued the war against Cnossus, Gortyna, Aptera, and Eleuthernae. The Cnossian

* Not only the Europa type, but also the border of rays is characteristic of the money of Gortyna.

party was aided by Aetolian auxiliaries, and the Polyrhenians consequently turned for aid to Philip V. of Macedon, the enemy of the Aetolians. A reinforcement was despatched by Philip, and the Polyrhenian league was victorious.*

Period IV. circ. B.C. 200—67.

It is reasonable to suppose that the Cretan cities, with rare exceptions to be noted under Period V., lost the right of issuing money after the conquest of the island by Metellus in B.C. 67. That date has therefore been selected as the downward limit for the purely autonomous coinages of Crete. Coins of several cities seem on grounds of style and of weight (light Attic) to belong to the fourth period. The silver coins which exactly reproduce the familiar types of the later Athenian tetradrachms (*obv.* Head of Pallas, *rev.* Owl on amphora), but which bear the names and badges of Cretan cities, doubtless belong to the beginning of this period (see pl. vi. 4; vii. 15; xi. 6; xvii. 2; xviii. 11). Several coins of this class have been published by M. Beulé (*Mon. d'Athènes*, pp. 90, 91) and by Mr. R. Stuart Poole (*Num. Chron.* N. S. i. p. 174; see also Wroth, *Cretan Coins*, pp. 26—28). Specimens issued by six Cretan cities are extant—Cnossus, Cydonia, Gortyna, Hierapytna, Polyrhenium and Priansus. Beulé and Poole suggest that these specimens were minted at the time when the Cretans were in

* Cf. Thénon in *Rev. arch.*, xv. N. S. p. 426. When Lyttus was destroyed by the Cnossians in B.C. 220, its inhabitants took refuge at Lappa. It has been supposed by some critics that Lyttus was soon rebuilt, and it was certainly inhabited at the time of the Roman conquest of Crete (B.C. 67), and at a later date. None of its extant money need, on grounds of style, be necessarily assigned to a later date than B.C. 220, and it would seem that after its destruction no more autonomous coins were issued. There appears to be no Imperial money of the place, unless the coin of Caligula and Germanicus described by Mionnet, Sup. vol. iv. p. 329, no. 214, be really of Lyttus. The coinage of Chersonesus seems to come to an end at the same time as that of Lyttus, of which city it was the port (cf. pl. iv. no. 5 with pl. xiv. no. 4).

alliance with Athens against Philip V.—an alliance brought about by Cephisodorus, *circ.* B.C. 200. Mr. Head (*Guide*, vi. B. 30) supposes that the Athenian types were simply adopted for commercial reasons, and this theory is also hinted at by Beulé as an alternative.* Some of the heads of Pallas on the obverse of these pieces are of the ordinary style of the later Athenian tetradrachms (e.g. at Cnossus, pl. vi. no. 4 = Head, *Guide*, pl. 56, 30), while others are somewhat barbarous, and betray the hand of unskilful Cretan workmen (e.g. Polyrhenium, pl. xvii. no. 2, and Priansus, pl. xviii. no. 11 = *Num. Chron.* N.S. i. pl. vii. figs. 2, 3).

Period V. B.C. 67—27 and Period VI. The Empire.

From B.C. 67 till the accession of Augustus to the Empire some limited issues of money in Crete were permitted by the Romans, but they were probably confined to two cities, Cnossus and Gortyna. The earliest of the coins that fall within this period is the interesting tetradrachm of Gortyna, published, with an engraving, by Dr. J. Friedlaender in the tenth volume of the *Zeitschrift für Numismatik* (1883), p. 119 ff. Its obverse bears a helmeted head of Roma, its reverse, the Ephesian Artemis and the legend ΓΟΡΤΥΝ. The elephant's head, which appears in the field of the reverse, and also as an ornamentation of the helmet of Roma, is evidently, as Dr. Friedlaender has pointed out, the badge of Q. Caecilius Metellus; and the coin must have been struck during the period when Metellus, after winning by his conquest the appellation 'Creticus,' was engaged in organizing the island as a Roman Province, B.C. 67—66. The following remarkable Cistophorus, published by Dr. Imhoof-Blumer (*Monn. Gr.* p. 210), was probably likewise issued at Gortyna, and belongs to the period B.C. 67—B.C. 31:—

* Cp. also F. Lenormant, *Monnaies et Médailles* (Paris, Quantin), p. 145.

"Æ 26m. Grammes 11,90.—Au milieu d'une couronne de lierre, une *ciste* entr'ouverte, d'où s'échappe un *serpent* à g.

℞. Entre deux *serpents*, dressés et affrontés, Zeus Krétagénès nu debout à dr., lançant le foudre de la main dr., et tenant sur la gauche un aigle qui s'envole à dr. Au-dessus **ΚΥΔΑΣ**; dessous **ΚΡΗΤΑΡΧ—ΑΣ**;* dans le champ, **ΚΡΗ—ΤΑΙ**
Ε — Ω
Ν.

Mus. nat. de Naples, no. 7581 du Catalogue, où la légende est erronément reproduite par **ΚΡΗΤΑΙΩΝ** et **Ε** dans le champ;—

Cab. de France, gr. 11,37."

(Cp. also Goltz, *Insulae*, pl. iv. and Pinder, *Ueber die Cistophoren*, 1856, p. 564).

Besides this Cistophorus, and the tetradrachm of Gortyna already referred to, some copper coins of Cnossus belong to this period. After the conquest of Crete, and probably before the battle of Actium, Cnossus became a Roman Colony with the name "Colonia Julia nobilis Cnossus" (or Gnosus). A list of its colonial coins is given by Dr. Imhoof-Blumer in his *Monnaies grecques*, pp. 213, 214 (compare p. 26, nos. 71—77, of this *Catalogue*). The coinage of Crete bearing the heads of Emperors is not well represented in the British Museum. The coins are of silver and copper, and range in date from Augustus to the Antonines: they are inscribed (1) with the names of Cretan towns (generally in an abbreviated form), or (2) with the words **ΚΟΙΝΟΝ ΚΡΗΤΩΝ** or **Κ Κ**. Other specimens give no indication of their mint-place. Coins of the first-named class (with the name of towns) were issued by some seven or more cities—Axus, Cydonia, Eleuthernae, Gortyna, Hierapytna, Lappa, Polyrhenium.†

* Κρητάρχης "implique l'existence d'un *κοινὸν τῶν Κρηταιέων* dont Κύδας était le président .... le **ΚΟΙΝΟΝ ΚΡΗΤΩΝ** des monnaies du temps de l'Empire." Imhoof-Blumer, *loc. cit.* Cp. Perrot, in Daremberg and Saglio, *Dict. des ant.*, *s. v.* 'Cretarcha.'

† Itanus and Lyttus seem somewhat doubtful; see Mion. *Sup.* iv. 325, 193;

The strange and well-marked character of the art of Cretan coins was long ago noted by Eckhel. Mr. R. Stuart Poole, in a Lecture delivered at the Royal Institution in 1864,* was the first to call attention to the merits this art possesses. The Cretan artist goes straight to nature for his inspiration: he excels, as Mr. Poole has pointed out, "in the portrayal of animal and vegetable subjects, and delights in perspective and fore-shortening." Some further suggestive criticism has been advanced by Prof. Gardner in his work on the *Types of Greek Coins*.† One remark there made ought especially to be borne in mind when viewing Cretan coins from the artistic point of view, namely, that the love of nature and the picturesque which are conspicuous in Cretan coin-art, are, to some extent, the result of the *religious* conditions under which the artist worked. His task was to give artistic shape to a bizarre local mythology which was often associated with a somewhat crude nature-worship. Those trees, for instance, which he so often introduces are not inserted primarily as ornamental accessories, but as integral parts of the type, to give an outward expression to a religious belief. He does not, for example, on the coins of Gortyna, seat his Europa in a tree purely for the sake of artistic effect, but because the Gortynians venerated a sacred tree—that *juxta fontem platanus nunquam folia dimittens* which was the witness of the loves of Zeus and Europa.

The Art of Cretan Coins.

But although to a great extent conditioned by the peculiar

329, 214. The coins attributed by Sestini (see Mion. *Sup.* iv. pp. 343–349), Kenner (*Die Münzsamml. d. Stiftes St. Flor.*, p. 101 f.), and Leake (*Num. Hell.* s. v. Thalassa) to 'Thalassa' have not been included in this Catalogue (see Wroth, *Cretan Coins*, pp. 56—58): the coins of Vespasian (p. 3 nos. 13, 14) are evidently of Crete *in gen.*, though classed by Sestini with the Thalassa coins (see Mion. *Sup.* iv. pp. 345, 346).

* Published in *Num. Chron.*, 1864, p. 240; cp. also *Encyclop. Britannica*, 8th and 9th eds., art. 'Numismatics.'

† Pp. 160—167, and cp. pl. ix., and p. 172.

character of Cretan myths, the art of Crete as displayed on its coins, has certainly originality and even charm. The Cretan coin-types are interesting, moreover, as exponents of certain qualities displayed by this local school of Greek art of which, otherwise, we should know almost nothing. It is, however, fairly open to question whether these very qualities of picturesqueness and uncompromising realism are those which we most desire for coin-reliefs. Now, on comparing the work of a Cretan coin-engraver with that of a good Greek coin-engraver who is not of Crete, what we are almost compelled to decide is, that the designs of the Cretan artist are indeed excellent in themselves, but that the designs of the non-Cretan artist are not only excellent absolutely, but relatively, and are peculiarly fitted for the purpose for which they are employed. The Cretans, in fact, seem to have lacked that sense of fitness, that habitual recollection of the material conditions under which they worked, which is one of the leading characteristics of Greek coin-engravers, indeed of all Greek artists. In their love of natural objects pure and simple, they forgot that natural objects fastidiously selected and even conventionalized may, under some conditions, be more artistically satisfying than nature faithfully transcribed from field and wood; and thus, though the bull on the coins of Gortyna (pll. ix. x. of this Catalogue) may be nearer nature than the bull on the coins of Thurium (Gardner, *Types*, pl. v. no. 24), the *θούριος βοῦς* must be pronounced the finer coin-type.

All the foregoing remarks of course apply only to those Cretan coins which are fairly well designed and executed; for, as numismatists are aware, there are many specimens in the series which are altogether beneath criticism. Some of these latter are simply the product of barbarous workmen who cannot make visible even the distinction between the male and female head; while many others, though better executed, betray an undoubted substratum of bar-

barism. Inequalities in the technical execution of contemporaneously issued coins are common enough in almost any Greek city, but they are particularly glaring in Crete. It seems that we may trace in most of the Cretan coins, especially in the period B.C. 431—300, three distinct styles of coin-engraving, all apparently contemporary. First, we have the coin of creditable design and execution serving as a model for the Cretan mints; next, there is the tolerably faithful though unskilled imitation of this prototype; while, finally, we have the rudest attempts at reproduction by an utterly barbarous hand. These differences may be well seen on the obverse of three coins of Gortyna photographed in pl. ix. The obverse of no. 5, both for grace of design and delicacy of execution, is worthy of all praise. The next specimen (no. 6, cp. no. 7) successfully reproduces the original motive, but the delicacy of execution is gone; while the third engraver, as a glance at the plate will show (ix. 10), is only competent to design for us a blurred figure of uncertain sex perched in a tree of laths. Sometimes, though not very frequently, the Cretans used the coins of other Greek cities as patterns from which to copy direct; in some instances with considerable success, as in the Hera of Cnossus (pl. v. 11, 12) modelled on the Hera of the later (fourth century) coins of Argos; though in other cases with disastrous results, as in the coins of Chersonesus (pl. iv. 2, 3, cp. *obv.* of no. 1), which are imitated from the fine money of Stymphalus in Arcadia.

Engravers' names.

We are made acquainted through extant coins with the names of two Cretan engravers—Neuantos and Pythodoros. The signature of Neuantos—ΝΕΥΑΝΤΟΣ ΕΓΟΕΙ—appears on the obverse of a didrachm of Cydonia, belonging to the end of the fifth or the beginning of the fourth century B.C. (see Mionnet, ii., p. 271, no. 112; engraved *Sup.* vol. iv. pl. ix. 2). No specimen of this coin is in the British Museum; but the obverse of the Cydonian coin photographed in our plate vii., no. 1, is almost identical in style with the obverse of the coin signed by Neuantos, and there can be little doubt that it is from his hand. It has been suggested that the monogram behind the head* (pl. vii. no. 1) is that of an engraver distinct from Neuantos. The objections to this theory are (1) that the head is in style almost identical with that on the specimen which bears the signature of Neuantos; (2) that the Cretan coin-artists never, so far as our evidence entitles us to judge, sign their names in monogram, but in full; (3) that the monogram is more easily explained as being that of a magistrate.

The signature of Pythodoros† occurs on the obverse of coins of Aptera (see pl. ii. no. 3; also Mionnet, *Sup.* vol. iv. pl. vii. no. 3= Wroth, *Cretan Coins*, pl. i. no. 4). This artist is evidently the same Pythodoros who worked for the not far distant town of Polyrhenium. We know the character of his work at Polyrhenium from coins in the British Museum (pl. xvi. no. 11; cp. p. 66), and elsewhere (Imhoof-Blumer, *Monnaies grecques*, p. 218, nos. 36, 37) bearing his signature on the obverse. On the specimens made by him for Aptera and Polyrhenium the female head is treated in a uniform style. The work (which closely resembles that of Neuantos) gives evidence of undoubted technical skill, but shows a tendency to be over-ornate.

It thus appears that the signed coins of Crete belong to a region of no great extent in the north-western part of the island; to Aptera, Polyrhenium, and Cydonia. Neuantos and Pythodoros were doubtless contemporaries; but whether they worked independently or were related to one another as master and pupil we

* This monogram has been variously read: see Sallet, *Zeit. f. Num.* ii. 7.

† This must be regarded as the true reading of the name: see Wroth, *Cretan Coins*, p. 13.

cannot determine. It is also uncertain whether these artists are responsible for the *reverse* types of coins which bear their signatures on the obverse. The reverse of the Aptera coin with the obverse signed by Pythodoros (pl. ii. 3), though of much mythological interest, is not very successful, artistically. The reverse type of the signed coin of Neuantos (Mion. *Sup.* vol. iv. pl. ix. 2; cf. our pl. vii. 1) is, on the other hand, a more creditable effort.

The female head on an unsigned silver coin of Polyrhenium (pl. xvi. 12) is, perhaps, also by Pythodoros: the well-executed copper coin of Aptera (pl. ii. 7) may with more confidence be attributed to him.

Cretan Coin-types

The Cretan types are eminently interesting on account of the information they furnish respecting the local mythology and religion. Many of the coins present us with purely Cretan divinities, while others, though portraying divinities worshipped throughout the Hellenic world, portray them under a more or less local form. The two male divinities who are represented most frequently on Cretan coins, either in person or by symbols, are Zeus and Apollo.

a. The chief Greek divinities.

The close connection of Zeus with Crete—there was his birthplace and his place of sepulture—is well known, and has been treated at length by Meursius (*Creta*, p. 71 ff.) and Hoeck (*Kreta*, i. p. 160 f.; cp. Ernst Fabricius, 'Die Idäische Zeusgrotte' in the *Mittheilungen des deutschen archäol. Institutes in Athen* (1885), vol. x. p. 59 ff.). The enthroned Zeus, holding sceptre and eagle, on the coins of Praesus (pl. xvii. 8, 9) is doubtless the Zeus called Diktaios, who is known to have possessed a temple in the Praesian territory (Strabo, x. 475).* On the coins of the Cretan Arcadia (pl. iii. 7)

* The Zeus on coins of Olus (pl. xiv. 12) may be the Zeus Tallaeus of the place (see *Bull de Corr. hell.*, iii., p. 293).

and Cnossus (pl. vi. 9) Zeus appears in the form of Zeus Ammon. The eagle (for example, at Lyttus and Itanus) is an obvious symbol of Zeus, and it is possible that the bee which appears on the coins of Aptera, Elyrus, Hyrtacina, and Praesus, may also be symbolic of the god, for in the legend of his infancy bees play a part of some importance (Diod. Sic., v. 70; Antonin. Liberalis, *Metam.* xix.; Callim. *Hymn. in Jov.* 47; Apollod. i. 1, § 3; cp. Meursius, *Creta,* p. 98 f.; Hoeck, *Kreta,* i., p. 177 f. and 186 f.). It would be natural to regard the bee as the symbol of the Ephesian Artemis, but that goddess does not seem to have been worshipped by the Cretans, and only appears quite exceptionally upon their coins (see *Zeit. f. Num.* x. 119 f.).

The goddess Hera seldom occurs: her appearance on the coins of Cnossus (pl. v. 11, 12) finds its explanation in the fact that it was in the neighbourhood of that city that her marriage with Zeus took place; an event afterwards commemorated by annual sacrifices and by a mimetic representation (Diod. Sic. v. 72; Pashley, *Travels,* i. p. 204).

Apollo appears very frequently, represented in the way usual in Greek art, or indicated by his Tripod. On several coins, however, he seems to be represented in the character of a hunter. On those of Eleuthernae we often find an undraped youthful figure, holding in one hand a bow, in the other a stone (pl. viii., nos. 5, 6, 7, 8, 10, 11). M. Fr. Lenormant (*Rev. Num.,* 1883, pp. 129—132) considered that in this class of representations we ought to recognize a Cretan hunter. It would rather appear, however, that the personage intended is Apollo himself, a hunter and patron of hunters. The earliest of all the coins of Eleuthernae* transports

* In the French collection. Photographed in Wroth, *Cretan Coins,* pl. ii. 5; see also Muret in *Revue Num.* (1883), i. p. 65, and Lenormant, *l.c.*

us at once to the forest, and shows us, though in a crude design, the divine hunter and huntress following their favourite pursuit; for hunting itself, as Xenophon* will have it, is the invention and delight of gods—Ἀπόλλωνος γὰρ καὶ Ἀρτέμιδος ἄγραι καὶ κύνες. The female figure of the obverse shooting with her bow, and attended by a hunting dog, cannot fail to be recognized as the Cretan Artemis (Diktynna or Britomartis: cp. C. I. G. 2566), and it is natural to suppose that the male personage occupying the reverse is her brother, Apollo, who seems to be clad in a short hunting tunic. He is advancing rapidly in pursuit of his prey, holding in his left hand a stone, in his right his bow: a hound runs on before him, and forest-scenery seems to be indicated by the presence of two trees. As already stated, a youthful figure holding a round stone and bow is a common coin-type at Eleuthernae, and appears also at the neighbouring town, Rhithymna (pl. xix. 8). The bow held by the figure would be suitable either to Apollo or to a mortal Cretan hunter, but the round stone is at Eleuthernae distinctly an attribute of Apollo, for on later bronze coins of the place (pl. viii. 13) we find an unmistakeable Apollo seated on the omphalos, beside which is a lyre, and holding in his outstretched right hand a round stone, his bow and quiver at his shoulder. The head of a laureate Apollo, moreover, is common on both silver and bronze coins of Eleuthernae (pl. viii. 6, 8), and occurs also at Rhithymna (pl. xix. 8). This type of a youthful figure holding stone and bow can hardly be discussed without taking into account a similar type which occurs on the reverse of coins of Tylisus, that of a naked youthful figure with long hair, holding in one hand a goat's head, and in the other a bow (pl. xix. 15). The analogy of the Eleuthernian coins would incline us to see in this figure a representation of Apollo, and there are positive

* *De Venat.* i. 1.

indications that Apollo is intended. It will be observed that in the field of this coin there appears an arrow-head: now, this object ought not to be regarded as an isolated symbol denoting a magistrate, but as having reference to the type itself, and especially to the goat's head, for on a silver coin of Praesus (pl. xvii. 10) we find as the type a half-goat, and in the field an arrow-head. On coins of Elyrus also (pl. viii. 15), and on those of Hyrtacina (pl. xii. 5) the type is a goat's head with an arrow-head beneath it. That the goat and arrow-head are connected with Apollo seems probable, because on the obverse of the coin of Praesus (pl. xvii. 10) is a head of that god, and on the reverse of another coin of the place (pl. xviii. 2) we find a goat's head placed within a laurel wreath, the obverse-type being, again, a head of Apollo. The Elyrus goat (pl. viii. 15) would also seem to be connected with Apollo, for (according to Pausanias, x. 16) there was at Delphi a brazen goat dedicated by the people of Elyrus, and represented suckling the infants Phylacis and Phylandros, who were children of Apollo by Acacallis.* All these indications lead us to infer therefore that the types which we have been discussing relate to Apollo in the character of a hunter, especially as a hunter of the famous wild goats of Crete, which, as modern travellers tell us, might still tax the energies of a mighty hunter (Spratt, *Travels*, i. pp. 12, 13).

Among well-known Hellenic divinities there occur on Cretan coins, Artemis, Herakles, Pallas, Hermes, Poseidon,† Dionysos, and Demeter,‡ or, possibly, Persephone. The Cretan Artemis has been

* Cp. also the coin of Ceraitae (Mion. ii. p. 264), *obv.* Head of Artemis or Apollo (?), *rev.* Spear-head and arrow-head.

† On Poseidon at Rhaucus: cp. Gardner, *Types*, p. 161.

‡ On the connection of Demeter with Crete, see Lenormant, art. 'Ceres' in Daremberg and Saglio, *Dict. des ant.*, p. 1029: she was particularly connected with Cnossus, and probably appears on its coins: see, *e.g.*, *infra*, page 19, no. 10.

treated of by Hoeck (*Kreta*, ii. p. 158 ff.) and by Lenormant (in Daremberg and Saglio, *Dict. des ant.*, s.v. 'Britomartis'). She was worshipped in some parts of the island under the names of Britomartis and Diktynna, and appears to have been a native goddess of hunters and fishermen, having also, perhaps, a lunar character. She was more or less assimilated to the Hellenic Artemis, and is represented as Artemis on coins of Cydonia (see pl. vii. 16). At Chersonesus there was a temple of Britomartis (Strabo, x. p. 479), and no doubt the female head which appears on the coins of that place (pl. iv. 1, 2) was considered by the inhabitants to be the head of Britomartis, though it was copied from coins of Stymphalus bearing the head of the Stymphalian Artemis. The city of Olus likewise possessed a sanctuary of Britomartis, as well as a wooden image of her attributed to Daedalus (Paus. x. 40, 3): the female head on its coins (pl. xiv. 12, 13) is evidently the head of the goddess. At Cydonia, Phalasarna, and Polyrhenium, the Cretan Artemis was venerated as 'Diktynna,' and her effigy appears on the coins of these cities (pll. vii. 16; xvi. 7, 8, 9; and xvi. 11, 12): on a Roman coin of Crete *in genere*, Diktynna is represented as the nurse of the infant Zeus (pl. i. 9). The city of Aptera appears to have had a local Artemis peculiar to itself (see pl. ii. and Lebas and Waddington, *Voyage arch.* (inscr.) tom. iii., p. 37, no. 75:—*τὸ ἱερὸν τὸ τᾶς Ἀρτέμιδος τᾶς Ἀπτέρας*).

Herakles occurs at several cities, notably at Phaestus, where he is represented in a variety of types (pl. xv. 1—9). We do not learn from other sources that he was held in especial honour at this city, though the eponymous hero, Phaestus, is recorded to have been related to him (Steph. Byz. s.v. *Φαιστός*; Paus. ii. 6, 7; ii. 10, 1). Hermes, who occurs on the coins of Aptera (pl. ii. 11), Gortyna (page 45, no. 62), Latus, (pl. xiii. 10), Phaestus (pl. xiv. 16), and Sybrita (pl. xix. 12, 13), is known also from extant inscriptions (*e.g.* C.I.G., no. 2554) to have been one of the divinities worshipped in Crete. In the Hermes on the coins of Gortyna we may perhaps recognize the local 'Hermes Hedas' mentioned in the *Etymologicum Magnum*, p. 315, 28.

β. Local Heroes and Divinities. Apteros or Pteras.

On several of the reverses of the coins of Aptera is the representation of a warrior either wholly or partially armed. On the later coins of the place (pl. ii. 8, 10) he is represented simply moving towards the left or facing; but on the earlier specimens (pl. ii. 3, 4, 5) he stands with one hand upraised before a tree. The word ΓΤΟΛΙΟΙΚΟΣ — on some specimens, ΓΤΟΛΙΟΙΤΟΣ,* — which seems to relate to the personage near whose figure it is written, is not known to occur elsewhere, either as a personal-name or as a descriptive epithet. It has been explained as equivalent to πολιοῦχος, 'Guardian of the City' (Raoul-Rochette, *Lettre . . . sur les graveurs*, &c., p. 5), or to πόλεως οἰκίστης, 'Founder of the City' (Leake, *Num. Hell.*, 'Aptera'). Either of these renderings of the word, and especially the latter, would induce us to recognize in the figure the eponymous hero of Aptera, who, according to Eusebius, bore the name of Apteras, and who was, moreover, a king of Crete. Parthenius, in his treatise περὶ ἐρωτικῶν παθημάτων (cap. xxxv.), also speaks of this personage (called by him Apteros) as a prince of the Cretans, but tells us nothing that throws light upon his connection with Aptera. The sturdy warrior of the coins may well be this Cretan chieftain, held in especial honour by the people of Aptera as the founder of their city. The tree with which the warrior is, by the action of his right hand, brought into close connection, remains to be explained. Its foliage (like that of the Gortynian 'platanus,' pll. ix. x.) is variously

* *Mus. Neap.*, 7607; cp. *Mus. Hunter.*, pl. iv. 13, with ΓΤΟΛΙΟΣΤΟΥ.

represented; but to judge from our pl. ii. no. 5, a laurel is intended. The warrior is not engaged (as has been sometimes said) in the rather meaningless action of plucking a leaf, but is portrayed in the act of adoring a sacred tree or some divinity of whom the tree is symbolical. The upraised hand is well known to have been the ordinary Greek gesture of adoration, and on an imperial coin of Pergamon (*Num. Chron.*, 3rd ser. ii. pl. iii. 7) the Emperor Caracalla may be seen saluting in the same manner a tree round which is coiled the serpent representative of Asklepios. The tree on the coins of Aptera may be a purely local object of worship, but a passage in Pausanias renders it more probable that it is the laurel of the Delphian Apollo which is here intended. According to a story which Pausanias (x. 5, 9 and 10) had heard, the founder of the Cretan city Aptera was Pteras, a Delphian who built the second temple of Apollo at Delphi. This Pteras is no doubt the same person as Apteros, and it would thus appear that the founder of Aptera was in legend, or in historical reality, brought into close relations with Apollo, and in this way our type would find a probable explanation.*

Velchanos.

The obverse type of pl. xv. 10, 12, has been discussed by several writers: Cavedoni, *Bulletino*, 1841, on R. P. Secche, '*Giove* Ϝέλχανος;' Welcker, *Griech. Götterl.*, ii. p. 244 f.; Stephani in *Compte-rendu*, St. Petersburg, 1866, p. 127; Friedlaender, *Annali*, xviii., p. 154; *Revue num.*, 1842, p. 82; 1844, p. 313); among them, Overbeck, who, in his *Kunstmythologie* (vol. ii. 'Zeus,' p. 197), accepts the identification of the youthful seated figure with a Cretan Zeus 'Velchanos.' This identification rests on a passage in Hesychius in which the

* The type has been previously discussed by Leake, *Num. Hell.*, 'Aptera'; Gardner, *Types*, p. 164, and by the present writer, *Cretan Coins*, p. 14.

word Γέλχανος (probably intended for Ϝέλχανος) is explained as Ὁ Ζεὺς παρὰ Κρησίν.

Talos.

The representation of Talos on the coins of Phaestus (pl. xv. 11, xvi. 6) has been discussed by Cavedoni, *Annali*, vii. p. 154 ff.; Baron de Witte, in the *Revue numismatique*, 1840, p. 188 ff.; Wroth, *Cretan Coins*, p. 51; cp. Hoeck, ii. p. 70 ff. It should be noticed that on the silver coins the name is given as ΤΑΛΩΝ, not ΤΑΛΩΣ as in the Authors, and that the figure is provided with wings, a detail not mentioned by the mythographers. In pl. xvi. 6, we see, on the obverse, this winged guardian of Crete, whose function was periodically to traverse the island; on the reverse, the golden Dog, made, as was the Man of Brass himself, by the god Hephaestos, and set as a protector to the infant Zeus in Crete, and afterwards to a Cretan Temple of Zeus. Talos is represented rushing forward, hurling a stone, perhaps to oppose the landing of the Argonauts or of some other strangers who are nearing the shore.

Zeus and Persephone at Priansus.

The curious obverse-type of the coins of Priansus in pl. xviii. 6, seems at first sight to be 'Hygieia and her serpent.' But though the serpent is a constant companion of Hygieia, not all serpents are Hygieian, and we must beware (as Stephani, *Compte rendu*, St. Petersburg, 1860, p. 102, has remarked) lest we mistake some chthonic or other divinity for the veritable goddess of Health. Although it is just possible that the female figure in question may be Hygieia, whose father, Asklepios, was worshipped not far from Priansus, at Leben, it is much safer to adopt the interpretation proposed both by M. François Lenormant (*Gazette archéol.*, 1879, p. 24), and by Prof. Gardner (*Types*, p. 162), and to see on the coins a representation of Persephone, and of Zeus, who visited the goddess under the form of a serpent, when she became by him the mother of the Cretan Zagreus.* It should be noted that the date-tree, beneath which the female figure sits, is not merely an ornamental accessory, for it appears by itself *as the type* of other coins of Priansus, and must have had some local significance.

Kydon.

The reverses of the earlier coins of Cydonia (pl. vii. 1—3, 5) display a youthful hunter (sometimes accompanied by a dog) in the act of stringing his bow. In Cretan types of this class it would generally seem (see above, p. xxvi) that we have a representation of the hunter Apollo. Here, however, the figure is probably the local hero, Kydon, who may have been venerated by the famous Cydonian bowmen† as the first great bowman of the city. The infant, suckled by an animal, the reverse type of other coins of Cydonia (pl. vii. 4, 7), may also be called Kydon, though no legends of his infancy are related in the Authors. According to a Cretan legend mentioned by Antoninus Liberalis (*Metam.*, cap. 30), Miletus, the son of Acacallis, daughter of Minos, was exposed when an infant, and was suckled by a wolf; and it is not unlikely that a similar story may have been told by the Cydonians concerning their hero, Kydon, who was (by Apollo or by Hermes) also a son of Acacallis.‡ The animal on the coins seems to be rather a bitch hound than (as it has been sometimes called) a wolf: a hound may easily have taken the place of the wolf in the local legend.

The familiar Cretan legends relating to the Minotaur and to

* Cp. Wroth, 'Hygieia' in *Journ. Hell. Stud*, 1884, vol. v. pp. 87, 88.

† Paus. viii. 53, 2; Steph. Byz. s.v. Κυδωνία; Claudian, *Histrix*, v. 46.

‡ At Elyrus, Acacallis abandoned Phylacis and Phylandros, her children by Apollo, to the motherly care of a goat (Paus. x. 16). A rare coin of Praesus, published by M. Babelon (*Rev. Num.*, 1885, p. 161; pl. viii. 8), has an obverse-type which should be compared with the reverse-types of Cydonia (pl. vii. 4, 7 of this Catalogue).

The Minotaur and Europa Legends.

Europa receive full illustration on the coins of Cnossus and Gortyna respectively. The Labyrinth, variously represented as of swastika form (pl. iv. 7, 11, &c.), square (pl. vi. 6) or circular (pl. vi. 5), is an almost constant type at Cnossus, and the Minotaur frequently appears, armed with a stone. The youthful head (pl. iv. 8) placed in a frame of the maeander pattern (the Labyrinth) is no doubt that of Theseus, whose short hair seems to be bound with a taenia, as (*e.g.*) on a kylix in the British Museum,* which represents the hero attacking the Minotaur. A unique coin of Cnossus (in the Berlin Museum) bearing the inscription ΜΙΝΩΣ, gives a representation of Minos, who appears as a Zeus-like figure, seated, and holding a sceptre (see *Zeit für Num.* vi. p. 232 f.; cp. Mion. ii. p. 266, no. 60). On other Cnossian coins it is doubtful whether the personage represented is Zeus or Minos, but probably it is the former who is intended.† Among the other divinities who appear on the coins of Cnossus are Apollo, Hera, and Demeter or Persephone.

The coinage of Gortyna (pll. ix.—xi.) is mainly devoted to Europa and the bull, though other local divinities also occur (Zeus, Hermes, Apollo, Artemis). A remarkable type also appears at Phaestus (pl. xiv. 16). The representation of Europa in ancient art has formed the subject of essays by Stephani and Otto Jahn, and is discussed in the *Kunstmythologie* of Overbeck (vol. ii., 'Zeus'), and in Gardner's *Types of Greek Coins*, pp. 164, 165.‡

* *Journal Hell. Stud.*, vol. ii., p. 57 f.; pl. x.

† See Wroth, *Cretan Coins*, pp. 22, 23.

‡ The didrachms and hemi-drachms (cp. pl. x. 9—11) of Cretan style and weight, which Dr. Imhoof-Blumer (*Monn. grecq.*, 1883, pp. 215, 216, 223) has rightly withdrawn from Euboea and given to Gortyna, bear what seems to be the head of Europa.

Attributions. A few of the attributions in this Catalogue call for a brief discussion.

The tetradrachm on pl. ii. 1, formerly given to Laconia, seems to be rightly assigned by Mr. Newton (*Num. Chron.*, vii. p. 114) to Allaria. **(1) Allaria.** The objection of M. Bompois, in his "Étude des portraits attribués à Cléomène III.," p. 32, (note), that the coin reads ΛΑ not ΑΛ, is rendered of slight importance when we bear in mind that the smaller coins of Allaria have sometimes a retrograde legend (see *infra*, p. 7, no. 2).

Eckhel (*Nummi veteres*, p. 144; *Doct. num. vet.* ii. p. 304), Leake (*Num. Hell.*, 'Arsinoe Cretae'), and other numismatists, **(2) Arsinoe.** have assigned to a Cretan town 'Arsinoe' coins similar to those described on p. 13; cp. pl. iii. nos. 9—11. It is convenient to catalogue the British Museum specimens under that heading, though the attribution is not absolutely certain. Col. Leake speaks of the specimens described by him as being "certainly Cretan," though without saying whether he makes this statement guided by a knowledge of their *provenance* or solely by style and type. No. 10, in pl. iii. of our Catalogue, has a decidedly Cretan appearance, and bears the inscription ΑΡΣΙ. A Cretan town named Arsinoe is only known to us from Stephanus, who mentions it (as the ninth) among the Greek localities of that name :—*Ἀρσινόη πόλις . . . ἐννάτη, Λύκτου*. From this passage we must gather that the place was a small town dependent upon, and situated near, the city of Lyttus. Berkel and Westerman * have indeed proposed to substitute *Λυκίας* (Lycia) for the difficult reading *Λύκτου*, but the reading *Λύκτου* is retained by Meineke. Eckhel (who considers Arsinoe to have been a Cretan town) conjectures that it acquired its name from Arsinoe, the wife of Ptolemy IV.,

* Wroth, *Cretan Coins*, p. 15 note.

Philopator, a sovereign who is known to have rebuilt the walls of Gortyna, and who may possibly have intervened in the affairs of other Cretan cities. The female head on p. 13, nos. 1—4 (pl. iii. 9, 11) is perhaps intended for a portrait, though it cannot be said to bear a very close resemblance to Arsinoe III., the wife of Philopator, or indeed, to any other Egyptian queen. If not a portrait, the head may be simply that of Artemis.

Dr. Imhoof-Blumer, in his *Monnaies grecques* (1883), p. 212, no. 5, assigns to Chersonesus the following copper coin:—

(3) Chersonesus.

"Æ. 28^{m}. Gr. 12,90.—Tête de Pallas à dr., coiffée d'un casque à aigrette. Bord aplati.

℞. Proue de navire ornée d'un foudre, à dr.; au-dessus ΣΩΣΙ-ΤΙΜΟΣ; dessous ΧΕ, et dans le champ à g. une rose."

(The British Museum possesses a similar specimen, size 1·05; the Χ below the prow, obscure).

There is also in the British Museum a coin similar in every respect to these two specimens, except that instead of ΧΕ beneath the prow are the letters Δ [monogram] (the monogram being somewhat obscure). In size and fabric these coins differ in a marked way from the copper coins of Crete current in the 4th and 3rd centuries B.C., nor does there seem to be any record of these or similar specimens having been found in that island.* The chief arguments in favour of the attribution to Chersonesus are (1) that the types of Pallas and prow occur on copper coins which are undoubtedly of Chersonesus, (2) that the letters ΧΕ indicate the name of the town. But in answer to this it must be urged that the head of Pallas and a prow being (taken separately) common types there is nothing

* The specimen with Δ [monogram] formerly belonged to Mr. Woodhouse, whose collection was formed during his residence in Corfu: the *provenance* of the other British Museum coin is not known.

in them which necessarily compels us to assign coins which bear them to Chersonesus, unless on other grounds this attribution seems probable. And with regard to the letters **XE**, the fact of their place being taken by **Δ K** on a specimen in every other respect similar, and issued under the same Magistrate (Sositimos), shows that **XE** cannot stand for the name of the town which issued the coin.

(4) Lyttus.

The earliest coins assigned to Lyttus in the present volume doubtless belong to the first half of the fifth century B.C., and are of a later date than the earliest coins of Cnossus, Gortyna, and Phaestus. Lyttus (or Lyctus) was however not less ancient than the last-mentioned cities (cp. *Il.* ii. 647; xvii. 611; Hesiod, *Theog.*, 417, 482), and it is therefore probable that, like them, it issued money in the sixth century B.C., or at any rate during the opening years of the fifth century. Friedlaender and von Sallet, in their Guide (*Das königliche Münzkabinet*, p. 54, nos. 12, 13), attribute to Lyttus the following early coins:—

"Silber. 13 mill: Lyttus auf Creta.—Eberkopf linkshin."
℞. Vertieftes Quadrat. 4, 15; 4,1 Grm."

The British Museum possesses several similar specimens, *e. g.*—

A. *Obv.* Boar's head r.
Rev. Rude incuse square.
Æ ·55. Wt. 64·5 grains. Brit. Mus. (from the Borrell Coll.): see *Num. Chron.*, 1884, p. 276, pl. xii. no. 10.

B. Similar; incuse square (divided ?) Fabric somewhat less lumpy.
Æ ·65. Wt. 64·4 grains. Brit. Mus. *Num. Chron.*, 1884, p. 277, pl. xii. no. 11 = Head, *Guide to the Coins of the Ancients*, I. A. 33; pl. iii. no. 33.

C. *Obv.* Boar's head r.
Rev. Incuse square.
Æ ·35. Wt. 7·2 grains. Brit. Mus. (from the Borrell Coll.).

These coins are undoubtedly of high antiquity, and 82 of them occurred in the Santorin Find (discovered in 1821) of seventh and sixth century coins (see *Num. Chron.* 1884, vol. iv. 3rd ser., pp. 269—280, 'The Santorin Find'). The type of the boar's head would be suitable to Lyttus, and Baron Prokesch-Osten states that he obtained ten specimens of this class direct, as it seems, from Crete (*Archäol. Zeitung*, 1847, p. 149). On the other hand it must be borne in mind (1) that the type of the boar's head is not confined to Lyttus (Mr. Head, *Guide* I. A. 35, attributes them, though with hesitation, to *Lycia;* cp. De Longpérier, *Revue Num.*, 1861, p. 425, no. 20); (2) that the Euboic weight of these pieces offers an obstacle to their attribution to a Cretan town, where we should expect the Aeginetic standard;* (3) that specimens have been found in other places besides Crete, for example, in Cyprus (*Catal.* Huber, no. 700); in Thera (the Santorin Find); and in Seriphos (Prokesch-Osten, *Nichbekannte europ-griech. Münzen*, pl. iii. nos. 50, 51, 'Lyttus;' where the boar's head on no. 50 has been mistaken for an eagle's head). In these circumstances it has appeared desirable to exclude the British Museum coins of this class from the present Catalogue.

(5) Naxos.

The specimens described on p. 59 of this volume were formerly attributed to one of the towns in Crete named Apollonia: the similar but *inscribed* specimens published in 1885 by Mons. P. Lambros, in the *Zeitschrift für Numismatik* (xiii. pp. 125—127), show that all the coins should be assigned to the Cretan town of Naxos.

* Mr. J. P. Six, who is in favour of the attribution to Lyttus, would remove this difficulty by treating the coins which weigh about 64 grains as *thirds* of an Aeginetic Stater. (Private letter to the Writer, July 1884).

THE AEGEAN ISLANDS.

The Aegean Islands.

THE Aegean Islands, the coinages of which are described in the present volume, are those to which the ancient geographers applied (though with considerable variations of usage*) the names of Cyclades and Sporades. The Cyclades consist of two main groups which lie (roughly speaking) parallel to one another. The first group, consisting of the islands of Ceos, Cythnos, Seriphos, and Siphnos, projects southwards from Attica; the second, consisting of Andros, Tenos, Myconos, and Delos, runs out into the sea from southern Euboea. These two groups are, as it were, united on the south by the islands of Paros and Naxos, while between Ceos and Cythnos on the west, and Andros, Tenos, and Myconos on the east, a further union is effected by means of the islands of Gyaros and Syros, which are placed like stepping-stones between them. South of Paros and Naxos lie the Sporades:—Melos, Thera, Cimolos (islands of volcanic nature), and Pholegandros, Sicinos, Ios, Amorgos, and Anaphe. A description of the coins of the islands in the north of the Aegean (Sciathos, Peparethos, &c.), and of those adjacent to the western coast of Asia Minor, does not come within the scope of this volume.

Their History.

The history of these islands, individually, is in most cases not fully known to us, but there are a few broad outlines in their history as a whole that can be fairly well made out.† At an early period, perhaps from about

* See Bursian, *Geographie von Griechenland*, ii. p. 348, note.

† For historical and geographical accounts of the islands, see chiefly A. Meliarakes, Κυκλαδικά, Athens, 1874; Bursian, *Geographie von Griechenland*, vol. ii. pp. 348—351; 438—529; L. Ross, *Reisen auf den griech. Inseln des*

900 to 700 B.C., we find them occupied by men of Ionian race,* and the sacred island of Delos stands out conspicuous as the scene of the great Panegyris frequented by Ionians from all the islands and coasts.† "It is in Delos," exclaims the Homeric Rhapsode, that the heart of Apollo most delights; for, "there in thy honour, Phoebus, the long-robed Ionians assemble, with their children and their gracious dames." "A man would say that they were strangers to death and old age evermore, who should come on the Ionians thus gathered: for he would see the goodliness of all the people, and would rejoice in his soul, beholding the men and the fairly-cinctured women, their swift ships and their mighty wealth." In time, when the Ionians of the Asiatic coast withdrew from the Delian festival, its glory declined, but Delos long maintained its sacred influence, and continued to attract the gifts of many worshippers. In the third and second centuries B.C., it became, moreover, an important centre of commerce.

Among the other islands which are prominent in the two centuries preceding the Persian Wars, Siphnos is remarkable for the riches derived from its mines of precious metal, and Thera for its early prosperity and for its foundation of the colony of Cyrene. Naxos, under its tyrant Lygdamis, attains the highest degree of power and wealth; Andros and Paros send out colonies to the Chacidice and to Thasos. At the time of the Persian invasion the Islanders made no united resistance, though some of them, like the people of Siphnos and Seriphos were found fighting on the side of the Greeks.

The rise of Athens to maritime supremacy, and the formation of the Confederacy of Delos, form an important landmark

ägäischen Meeres; L. Lacroix, *Iles de la Grèce*; T. Bent, *The Cyclades*. Meliarakes and Bursian give references to monographs on the different islands.

* Some of the Sporades (Melos, Thera, Anaphe, Pholegandros) were Doric.

† Cp. Jebb, "Delos," in *Journ. Hell. Stud.*, i. p. 17 ff.

in the history of the Aegean Islands; and during the fifth century B.C. we find them in a dependent condition, paying tribute to the Athenians (For the details of the Tribute-Lists see U. Köhler, *Urkunden und Untersuchungen zur Geschichte des delisch-attischen Bundes*, especially p. 196 ff.). From the fourth century onwards the Athenians are exchanged for a succession of other masters—Macedonian, Ptolemaic, Roman.* Andros, for instance, about B.C. 314, was compelled to receive a Macedonian garrison, from which it was temporarily freed by Ptolemy I. in B.C. 308. In B.C. 200 it was taken by Attalus, King of Pergamus, in alliance with the Romans, and in B.C. 133 passed into the possession of the latter along with the other Pergamene dominions. In B.C. 43 Antony gave the island (as well as Naxos and Tenos) to the Rhodians, from whom, however, it was soon withdrawn. Of Tenos, we hear that it was attacked by Alexander of Pherae in B.C. 362, and its inhabitants enslaved. Later on, it was one of the meeting places of the Island Confederation. The people of Siphnos and Cythnos are described by Demosthenes as living, in his time, the quiet, uninterrupted life of small and insignificant states. Under the Romans, some of the islands—Amorgos, Seriphos, Gyaros—acquire a grim importance from their being used as places of banishment. Of the relations of the Aegean Islands with the kings of Egypt we obtain some glimpses from certain inscriptions published by Boeckh (C. I. G. 2234, 2273, 2223*c*) and Homolle (*Bull. de Corr. hell.*, iv. 320 ff.). These inscriptions mention a Confederation of the Islanders (*κοινὸν τῶν νησιωτῶν*), and the celebration by it of a festival called *Ptolemaea*. It is evident that the Confederation was in constant relations with the sovereign of Egypt and his agents. So far as can be made out from the inscriptions,

* The islands also suffered much in the third century B.C., from the ravages of the Aetolians: see J. Martha in *Bull. de Corr. hell.*, ix. (1885), pp. 497, 498.

it dates from the early part of the third century B.C. (perhaps from the reign of Ptolemy Philadelphus, B.C. 285—247) and lasts till the end of that century, or perhaps a little later. It can hardly be doubted that it was politically dependent upon Egypt, and its functions seem to have been confined to the regulation of festivals and the decreeing of honorary rewards.

Periods of Coinage.

The coinage of the Aegean Islands divides itself into two large classes, the first, consisting of silver coins, is of archaic style, of the seventh and sixth centuries B.C.; the second, chiefly of copper, belongs, apparently, to a late time, probably to the second and first centuries B.C. During the fourth and third centuries, and still more during the fifth, the issue of money in the Aegean does not appear to have been plentiful, and in several islands does not take place at all. Under the Empire, a copper coinage of the ordinary "Greek Imperial" kind is current, though in no great abundance, in most of the islands. The present volume includes imperial coins of Amorgos (Minoa, pl. xx. 7), Andros, Gyaros (probably; pl. xxiii. 7), Ios (pl. xxiii. 14, 15), Melos, Myconos (pl. xxv. 5), Naxos, Paros, Siphnos (pl. xxvii. 16), Syros (pl. xxviii. 7, 8, 9), Tenos, and Thera (pl. xxix. 17, 18).

Early coinage.

The large hoard of 760 Greek silver coins discovered in Santorin (Thera) in the year 1821, contained specimens of the money which circulated in the Aegean during the seventh and sixth centuries B.C. A photographic plate showing specimens of the different types, and accompanied by a description of the coins based on a Memorandum as to the Find made at the time by Mr. Borrell, was published by the present writer in the *Numismatic Chronicle* for 1884 (vol. iv. 3rd ser. pp. 269—280; plate xii). Of these 760 coins, 541 were of Aegina; among the rest were specimens attributable almost with certainty to particular islands of the Aegean (Naxos, Paros, Siphnos), and these, and similar coins, will be found catalogued and illustrated in the present volume (pls. xxv. 7, 8; xxvi. 1; xxvii. 9). But the Santorin Find contained other coins, the exact attribution of which is doubtful, some being probably of Northern Greece, others of the Aegean Islands. To the class of island coins may belong the specimens numbered 6, 9, 12, and 17, in plate xii. of the *Num. Chronicle* (1884). It was not, however, deemed advisable to catalogue these coins here, as, until we obtain further evidence respecting their usual *provenance*, their attribution is to a great extent guess-work. The remarkable and unique coin (no. 17) with the head of a Seilenos or a Centaur might well be of the earliest mintage of Naxos, though at present we have no proof of this from Finds. No. 12, with *obv.* two Dolphins, has been attributed to Argos, to Delos, and to Thera: * specimens of it have been found in Aegina and Ceos† as well as in Thera. No. 6, with *obv.* Fish's head and tail, has been found in Melos and Thera. Specimens derived from the Santorin Find and from other sources, show that there was a currency of archaic style in the islands of Ceos, Naxos, Paros, and Siphnos. It is probable that certain other islands of the Aegean, especially Andros, Delos, Melos, and Thera, were not without coinages of their own, but the allotment of coins to them from extant specimens is very difficult.‡ This early island currency consists mainly of didrachms of Aeginetic weight, more or less globular in fabric; they bear some simple device (a goat, eagle,

* To Thera, by Mons. J. P. Six, in private letters to the Writer (23 March and 12 April, 1885).

† Brönsted, *Voyages et rech. en Grèce*, i. p. 63, note 1.

‡ The attribution to Melos of the coin in Friedlaender and von Sallet, *Das königliche Münzkabinet*, p. 54, no. 8, pl. i. 8 : (Apfel (μῆλον) mit zwei Blättern. ℞. Vertieftes Quadrat [divided into two oblong compartments] mit drei kleinen Ringeln verziert. Æ. 20 mill., 13·8 grm.) seems doubtful, especially because the reverse differs greatly from the reverses of those archaic coins which are certainly of the Aegean Islands.

cuttle-fish, kantharos, amphora, &c.) on the obverse, and their reverse is an incuse square, generally quartered and divided diagonally (see plates xxi. 7; xxii. 1; xxv. 7; xxvi. 1; xxvii. 9).*

Later Coinage.

The troubles of the Persian Wars, and the long period during which the Aegean Islands were in more or less complete subjection to Athens, seem to have been unfavourable to the appearance of currencies in the islands, and coins belonging to the fifth century, and, in a less degree, to the earlier part of the fourth, are rare. Almost exceptionally, the wealthy island of Siphnos issues some fine coins which, though archaic, show a distinct advance upon the primitive seventh and sixth century money of Siphnos itself and the other islands (cp. pl. xxvii. 11, 12 with pl. xxvii. 9, 10). These coins probably belong to the beginning of the fifth century, though they may possibly be somewhat older. The metallic sources of Siphnian wealth, however, became exhausted at a comparatively early period, and after issuing some copper coins of beautiful style, of the fourth century (pl. xxvii. 14, 15), the island seems to disappear from numismatic, as it does from political history, only to emerge with a feeble currency in

* The didrachms of the Santorin Find weigh as a rule from 180 to 194 grains; a few specimens, nos. 6, 9, 17, of pl. xii. of the *Num. Chron.*, 1884, weigh more than 194 grains (227, 223, 219, 216, 211, 208 grains). M. Six has drawn up (Letter of 23rd March, 1885) an instructive list of the coins of this Find arranged in two classes according to weight. All the coins of the first class weigh more than 200 grains (according to M. Six, "poids éginétique") and have as reverse an amorphous incuse square: those of the second class ("poids éginétique réduit") have the square more or less neatly quartered and divided diagonally. M. Six remarks that when the didrachms of the hoard were buried, "il y avait encore en circulation quelques rares exemplaires des statères du poid eginétique normal, non réduit, tandis que la grande masse consistait en statères, de poids réduit à celui de trois drachmes euboiques et au-dessous." He considers that we may assert that "le carrè creux simple, et sans divisions, finit quand le poids eginétique est réduit, et comme cette réduction doit avoir eu lieu avant Solon, il s'en suit que toutes ces pièces à ce carrè creux primitif sont anterieures au 6ᵉ. siècle et datent du 7ᵉ. siècle."

imperial times (pl. xxvii. 16). During part of the fourth century and during the third, a few important islands, Andros, Melos, Naxos, Paros, and Tenos, display something like a continuous coinage, consisting of silver (of Rhodian or of light Attic weight) as well as of copper coins. There seems to have been no mintage of tetradrachms with the types of Alexander. Certain Alexandrine coins bear symbols which correspond to the coin-types of the islands—the kantharos, bunch of grapes, thyrsus, lyre, bee, dolphin, harpa—but these symbols are not sufficiently distinctive to justify our appropriating the coins on which they occur to particular islands of the Aegean.* At some period or other nearly all the islands of the Aegean found an opportunity to coin money: it is hard, however, to discover the time when the goodwill or temporary absence of their various masters would have permitted them to exercise this prerogative. The coins of most of the less important islands are of copper and not of silver, and their arrangement on grounds of style is consequently not easy. Most of these copper currencies (as at Anaphe, Ceos, Cythnos, Pholegandros) have been in this *Catalogue* assigned to the second and first centuries B.C., though some may possibly be earlier. The insignificant copper coins of Delos (pl. xxiii. 1—6) were probably current chiefly during the first half of the second century B.C., as may be inferred from the mention in Delian inscriptions of that period of the *χαλκὸς Δήλιος* and *χαλκοῖ ἐπιχώριοι*:† it is unlikely that any of the coins are later than B.C. 87, when Menophanes, the general of Mithradates, ravaged the island, a disaster from which it never completely recovered.

* See Müller, *Num. d'Alexandre le grand*, pp. 226, 227.

† See Homolle in *Bull. de Corr. hell.*, ii. (1878), p. 578 f.; Jebb, "Delos," in *Journ. Hell. Stud.*, i. p. 57; Gardner, *Journ. Hell. Stud.*, 1883, "Votive coins in Delian inscriptions." On the copper coins whose issue Dr. Köhler would attribute to Athenian Kleruchs settled in Delos after B.C. 166, see *Mittheil. d. deut. Arch. Inst. in Athen*, vi. (1881), p. 238 ff.

Coin-types.

The chief divinity of the coinage of the wine-growing Isles of the Aegean is Dionysos. Naxos, that ancient and important centre of the Dionysiac cultus,* and Andros, where, at intervals, the fountain in the temple of the god is said to have miraculously flowed with wine,† abound in Dionysiac types; and, in fact, the same may be said of nearly all the other islands (Amorgos, Ceos, Cythnos, Melos, Myconos, Paros, Syros, Tenos, &c.). The head of the god is represented wreathed with ivy, and appears either as bearded or as youthful; both representations occurring on the coinages of one and the same island (*e.g.* at Andros (pl. xx. 10, 13), Ceos (pl. xxi. 23; xxii. 14), Myconos (pl. xxv. 1, 2). The symbols of Dionysos are extremely common as types, and are of the familiar kind—the kantharos (*e.g.* pl. xxv. 7), amphora (pl. xxi. 7), thyrsus (pl. xx. 15), bunch of grapes (pl. xxi. 13, 23), ivy-wreath (pl. xxvi. 7), and panther (pl. xx. 9).

Next to Dionysos, Apollo is probably the most important god on the coins. The types of the Delian money are devoted to him and to Artemis, (pl. xxiii. 1—6), the most interesting type being that of a palm-tree with a swan upon it (xxiii. 2). Both the swan and the palm-tree are well known to have been sacred to Apollo. It was under the shadow of a palm in Delos that Leto gave birth to her son; and, in historical times, we hear of Nicias dedicating a brazen palm-tree to the Delian god.‡ The Apollo who appears on the coins of Anaphe (xx. 8) is probably the Apollo "Aegletes" or "Asgelatas" of the place:§ in the Apollo on the money of Ceos and

* See Lenormant, art. "Bacchus," in Daremberg and Saglio, *Dict. des ant.*, p. 594*a*.

† Plin., *Hist. Nat.*, ii. 103, 231; Steph. Byz. *s.v.* Ἄνδρος; Paus., vi. 26, 2, &c.

‡ Cp. Leake, *Num. Hell.*, "Delus;" Daremberg and Saglio, *Dict. des ant.*, p. 317*a* (swan); *ib.* p. 358*b* (palm).

§ Bursian, *Geographie*, ii., p. 519.

Thera, we should, no doubt, recognize Apollo Smintheus and Apollo Karneios, respectively (Bursian, *Geog.* ii. pp. 472, 473, 527).

Pallas, Artemis,* Pan, and Zeus are represented on the coins; the last-named divinity at Tenos in the form of Zeus Ammon, bearded as well as youthful (pl. xxviii. 10, 19). Asklepios, though worshipped in some of the islands, appears very rarely on the coins, though the bearded and laureate head on the obverse of money of Amorgos (pl. xx. 1, 3), where the cupping vessel appears as the reverse type, may perhaps be his (cp. on these types, Lambros, *Νομίσματα τῆς νήσου Ἀμοργοῦ*, Athens, 1870). The coin of Paros (pl. xxvi. no. 10) representing a female figure seated on a *cista* and holding ears of corn and a sceptre, is in all probability intended for Demeter Thesmophoros, an important Parian goddess (see Lenormant, in Daremberg and Saglio, *Dict. des ant.*, p. 1029*b*): the conjecture (cp. Thiersch, *Über Paros und parische Inschriften*) that this figure is Cleoboia, the woman who introduced into Thasos from Paros the Mysteries of Demeter, and who was painted by Polygnotus in the Lesche at Delphi, seems a less probable one.† Poseidon is rare on the coins of the islands, though he is well represented at Tenos (pl. xxviii. 10, 14, 17, *reverses*) where there was a celebrated temple of the god situated in a grove,

* The head of 'Artemis?' at Siphnos (p. 121) is considered by R. Weil, *Hist. u. phil Aufsätze E. Curtius . . . gewidmet*, Berlin, 1884, p. 128) to be that of Apollo.

† Demeter is probably the goddess who is represented on the coin described on p. 84, no. 7, and there attributed (contrary to the opinion of Sestini, *Lett.*, vi. p. 39, and of Dr. Friedlaender, *Z. f. N.*, iv. 369) to Aegiale in Amorgos. This coin, both in the style of its lettering and in its thin flat fabric, bears a close resemblance to the Imperial coin of Minoa, in Amorgos (see below, p. 84, no. 9). Friedlaender (*l.c.*) has attributed it, as well as the following coins reading ЄΓΙΑΛЄΩΝ to Aegialus in Paphlagonia (cp. Sestini, *l.c.*):—(1) Æ. of Caracalla. ℞. Dionysos standing: published by P. Lambros in *Zeit. für Num.*, iii. p. 219, and attributed by him to Aegiale in Amorgos. (2) Æ. of Caracalla with the inscription ЄΠΙ ΑΡΧ ΠΡΥΤΑΝЄΙ ЄΠΙΚΡΑΤΟΥ Β ЄΓΙΑΛЄΩΝ and "Juno Pronuba" and "Apollo Didymeus," standing. Size, 34 millimètres. With regard

and much frequented by strangers at the time of festivals.* The dolphin and the cuttle-fish on the archaic coins of Ceos (pl. xxii. 1) are doubtless emblems of Poseidon or of some other marine divinity.

Among the types of especial local significance are the representations of Aristaeus in Ceos, of Homer in Ios, of Perseus in Seriphos, and of the Cabiri at Syros.† With the island of Ceos, Aristaeus was very closely connected. At a time when it was suffering from drought and pestilence, he appeared and sacrificed to Zeus Ikmaios, who caused refreshing breezes to blow for forty days. Aristaeus also instituted propitiatory sacrifices to the dog-star Sirius, and instructed the Cean Nymphs in bee-keeping and other arts. It is to Aristaeus that the star (pl. xxi. 25), the bee (pl. xxii. 12), and Sirius, the dog encircled by rays (pl. xxi. 22), make allusion on the coins of Ceos. In this island he was assimilated to Zeus and worshipped as *Ζεὺς Ἀρισταῖος*. The bearded head on the obverse of Cean coins (pl. xxi. 1—5) is therefore probably intended for Aristaeus: the youthful head (pl. xxi. 22, &c.), which occurs on other coins of Ceos, seems to be rather that of Apollo (a god much worshipped in the island), than a representation of Aristaeus as a youth (on Aristaeus at Ceos, see Roscher, *Lexicon der griech. u. römisch. Mythologie*,

to (2) Dr. Friedlaender urges that its size is an objection to its being assigned to Amorgos; but to this it must be answered that the island coins are by no means necessarily of small module, and the Brit. Mus. coin of Minoa in Amorgos, is itself about 30 millimètres in size. Moreover, the name and titles of a magistrate would hardly be expected on a coin of Paphlagonia, while, on the other hand, they certainly occur on coins of the Islands; in fact, the coin of Minoa just referred to bears a magistrate's name and the title of *archon*. Friedlaender asserts that no. 1, and the coin of Domna with Demeter in quadriga (p 84, no. 7, of this *Catalogue*), do not resemble in style and lettering the imperial coins of the islands; but an examination of the latter coins (which are more varied in fabric, style, and lettering, than Friedlaender would appear to assume) will not, we believe, bear out his assertion.

* Meliarakes, p. 14.

† On the Cabiri, at Syros, or rather the Cabiri assimilated to the Dioscuri, see Lenormant, art. "Cabiri," in Daremberg and Saglio, *Dict. des ant.*, p. 773.

p. 549; Daremberg and Saglio, *Dict. des ant.*, p. 424*b*; and Brönsted, *Voyages et recherches en Grèce*, vol. i.). The constant obverse type of the coins of Ios is the head of Homer (pl. xxiii. 8—13), whose burial-place was asserted to exist in the island (Pauly, *Real.-encyclop.*, s.v. "Ios"). The head is identified by the accompanying inscription ΟΜΗΡΟΥ, and appears first on a silver coin (there is no specimen in the British Museum) of the latter part of the fourth century B.C., a very early period for a numismatic representation of that kind (see Imhoof-Blumer, *Porträtköpfe auf antiken Münzen*, plate viii. no. 24, and Friedlaender, *Zeit. für Num.*, vol. i. p. 294). The beautiful head on the silver coin is well reproduced on the earliest of the copper coins (pl. xxiii. 8), which seem, however, from other considerations, not to be earlier than the second century B.C.

The coins of Seriphos are devoted to representations of Perseus and the Gorgon's head (pl. xxvii. 2—8), fitting devices in the island where legend said that the hero was brought up, and where he turned the inhabitants into stone * (Apollod., ii. 4 § 3; Pind., *Pyth.*, x. 72; xii. 18; Strab., x. p. 487; Ov., *Met.*, v. 242). It is stated by Pausanias (ii. 18. 1) that there was an important cultus of Perseus in Seriphos.

In concluding this Introduction, I am anxious to acknowledge my obligations to Mons. J. P. Six for a communication respecting the coins of the Santorin Find. I am also under a special obligation to Dr. Imhoof-Blumer with respect to the portion of this work which relates to Crete. After I had written the present Catalogue, and published a preliminary essay on "Cretan Coins," in the

* Mr. Bent (*The Cyclades*, p. 2) mentions that when on a recent visit to Seriphos, the peasants brought him specimens of the old coins with the Gorgon's head, and told him that they were "the coins of the first queen of Seriphos, who lived up at yonder castle."

Numismatic Chronicle, Dr. Imhoof-Blumer allowed me to take a copy of his complete and valuable manuscript catalogue of Cretan Coins, and I have therefore had the advantage of comparing my own conclusions with those of Dr. Imhoof-Blumer, and in certain instances of making corrections and modifications.

WARWICK WROTH.

CRETE.

CORRIGENDA.

Page 71, no. 10. *For* 'Dictaeus' *read* 'Diktaeus'.

Plate xxiii., no. 21. The reverse bears some resemblance to a bow-case, but the type intended is perhaps a Phrygian helmet, as described in the text (p. 103, no. 6). To correspond with that description the reverse on the Plate should be turned round.

Page 121. The object on the reverse of nos. 4—7 is probably a *leaf*, not a *barleycorn*.

CRETE.

No.	Wt.	Metal. Size.	Obverse.	Reverse.
			CRETE.	
			In genere.	
			SILVER AND BRONZE.	
			Caligula.	
1	118·3	Æ ·9	ΓΑΙΟΣ ΚΑΙΣΑΡ ΣΕΒ· ΓΕΡΜ · ΑΡΧ · ΜΕΓ · ΔΗΜ·ΕΞΟΥ·ΥΠΑ· Bust of Caligula r., bare; sceptre over left shoulder: border of dots.	Draped figure of Augustus, radiate, seated l. on curule chair, holding in r. patera, resting l. on sceptre; around him, seven stars: border of dots.
2	113·2	Æ ·95	Similar, but ΓΕΡ·	Similar. [Pl. I. 1.]
3	40·9	Æ ·65	Γ ΚΑΙΣΑΡ ΣΕΒ ΓΕΡ· ΑΡΧ ΜΕΓ · ΔΗΜ · ΕΞΟ · · · · Similar.	Bust of Augustus l., diademed and radiate; around, seven stars: border of dots. [Pl. I. 2.]
			Claudius.	
4	159·1	Æ ·95	[ΤΙ]ΚΛΑΥΔΙΟΣ ΚΑΙ-ΣΑΡ ΣΕ · ΓΕΡΜ · ΑΡΧ · · · · · · · · · · · · Head of Claudius l., bare: border of dots.	Car l. drawn by four elephants, on each of which is a driver; on car is a draped figure of Augustus, radiate, seated l.; above car, seven stars: border of dots. [Pl. I. 3.]
5	117·2	Æ 1·	ΤΙ ΚΛΑΥΔΙΟΣ ΚΑΙ-ΣΑΡ ΣΕ ΓΕΡΜ·ΑΡΧ· ΜΕΓ·ΔΗΜ · ΕΞΟΥ ΥΠ[Α] Similar.	Similar to no. 1.

No.	Wt.	Metal. Size.	Obverse.	Reverse.
			Claudius and Antonia (?).	
6		Æ ·8	[ΤΙ ΚΛΑΥΔΙ]ΟΣ ΚΑΙ-ΣΑΡ ΓΕΡΜ·ΣΕΒΑ· Head of Claudius l., bare.	ΘΕΑ ΣΕΒΑΣΤΑ Head of Antonia (?) r., wearing ornamented stephane. [Pl. I. 4.]
			Claudius, Antonia, and Drusus.	
7		Æ 1·05	ΤΙ·ΚΛΑΥΔΙΟΣ ΚΑΙ-ΣΑΡ ΓΕΡΜ·ΣΕΒΑΣ-ΤΟΣ Head of Claudius r., laur.	ΔΡΟΥ ΚΛΑΥ ΓΕΡ ΑΝΤΩΝΙΑ Head of Drusus l. bare, and of Antonia r., wearing veil and stephane. [Pl. I. 5.]
8		Æ 1·	Similar.	Similar.
			Claudius and Messalina.	
9		Æ ·8	[ΤΙ ΚΛΑΥΔΙΟΣ] ΚΑΙ-ΣΑΡ ΓΕΡΜΑ ΣΕΒΑ ... Head of Claudius l., bare.	[ΟΥΑΛ]ΕΡΙΑ ΜΕΣΣΑΛΕΙΝΑ Bust of Messalina r. [Pl. I. 6.]
10		Æ ·85	Similar.	Similar.
11		Æ ·85	Similar.	Similar.
			Claudius, Octavia, and Britannicus.	
12		Æ ·7	[ΑΥΤ ?] ΤΙ ΚΛΑΥ-ΔΙΟΣ ΓΕΡΜΑΝΙΚΟΣ Head of Claudius l., bare.	ΚΛΑΥ·ΟΚΤΑΙΑ·ΚΛΑΥ.... Busts jugate of Octavia and Britannicus r. [Pl. I. 7.]

No.	Wt.	Metal. Size.	Obverse.	Reverse.
			Vespasian.	
13		Æ 1·25	ΑΥΤΟΚΡΑΤΩΡ ΟΥΕΣΠΑΣΙΑΝΟΣ ΣΕ Head of Vespasian r., bare.	ΕΠΙΑΝΘΥΠΑΤΟΥΣΙΛΩΝΟΣ Male figure, radiate, standing l., his r. hand upraised, in his l. short sceptre; over his l. shoulder hangs chlamys. [Pl. I. 8.]
14		Æ 1·1	[ΑΥΤΟ]ΚΡΑΤΩΡ· ΟΥΕΣΠΑΣΙΑ[ΝΟΣ ΣΕ] Head of Vespasian r., laur.	[ΕΠΙ ΑΝΘΥΠΑ]ΤΟΥ [ΣΙΛΩ-ΝΟΣ] Zeus, wearing himation, seated l.; holding in r. thunderbolt, his l. resting on sceptre.
			Trajan.	
15	38·6	AR ·7	[IMP]CAES [NER T] RAIA OPTIM AVG GER DAC PART Bust of Trajan r., laur.	ΔΙΚΤΥΝΝΑ Diktynna, wearing drapery and endromides, seated l. on rocks; holding in r., javelin (?), and in l., infant Zeus; before her and behind her, one of the Curetes l. [Pl. I. 9.]
16	34·6	AR ·75	Similar (insc. complete).	ΔΙΚΤΥΝΝΑ ΚΡΗΤ Similar.
17		Æ 1·25	ΑΥΤΟΚΡΑΤωΡΑΥΓ· ΤΡΑΙΑΝΟ[C ΓΕΡ ΔΑΚΙ] Similar.	ΚΟΙΝΟΝ ΚΡΗ[ΤΩΝ] Zeus, wearing himation over lower limbs, seated l.; holding in r., Nike, in l., sceptre; at his feet, eagle.
18		Æ 1·25	[ΑΥΤΟΚ]ΡΑΤωΡ ΑΥΓ · ΤΡΑΙΑΝΟC ΓЄΡ · ΔΑΚ Bust of Trajan l., laur.	ΚΟΙΝΟΝ ΚΡΗΤωΝ Kybele, wearing turreted crown, seated l. on throne with back; in her r., patera; her l. rests on tympanon; on either side of throne, a seated lion.

No.	Wt.	Metal. Size.	Obverse.	Reverse.
19		Æ1·15	[ΑΥΤ]ΟΚΡΑΤωΡ ΑΥΓ· ΤΡΑΙΑ[ΝΟC ΓЄΡΔΑΚΙ] Bust of Trajan l., laur.	[ΚΟΙΝΟΝ] ΚΡΗΤωΝ Young Dionysos l., wearing short chiton and chlamys; holding in r., kantharos, in l., thyrsus reversed; at his feet, panther.
20		Æ1·25	[ΑΥΤΟΚΡΑΤωΡ] ΑΥΓ·ΤΡΑΙΑΝΟC ΓЄΡ·ΔΑΚ[Ι Similar.	Similar (inscr. complete).
21		Æ1·15	[ΑΥΤΟΚΡ]ΑΤωΡ [ΑΥΓΤΡΑΙΑΝΟC ΓЄΡ] Bust of Trajan l., laur.	ΚΟΙΝΟΝ ΚΡΗΤωΝ Diktynna, wearing short chiton, peplos and endromides, running r.; by her side, dog; in outstretched l. she holds bow, with r. draws arrow from quiver.
22		Æ1·12	ΑΥΤΟ[ΚΡΑΤΩΡΑΥΓ ΤΡΑ]ΙΑΝΟC ΓЄΡ ΔΑΚΙ Bust of Trajan r., laur.	ΚΡΗΤΩΝ ΚΟΙΝΟΝ Similar.
23		Æ1·	ΑΥΤ · ΑΥΓ ΤΡ[ΑΙ]-ΑΝΟC · ΓЄΡ · ΔΑΚΙ Bust of Trajan l., laur.	[ΚΟΙ]ΝΟΝ ΚΡΗΤωΝ Europa riding on bull r.; peplos flying.
24		Æ ·9	ΑΥΤΑΥΓ ΤΡΑΙΑΝΟC [ΓЄ]Ρ ΔΑΚ Similar.	[ΚΟΙΝΟΝ] ΚΡΗΤω[Ν] Zeus, wearing himation over lower limbs, seated l. on throne with back; holding in r., Nike, in l., sceptre; [at his feet, eagle].
25		Æ ·95	ΑΥ·ΤΡΑΙΑΝΟC ΓЄΡ Δ[Α]ΚΙΚΟ Bust of Trajan r., laur.	ΚΟΙΝΟΝ ΚΡΗΤΩΝ River-god with himation over lower limbs, reclining l.; holding in r., reed, l. resting on urn, from which water is flowing. [Pl. I. 11.]

No.	Wt.	Metal. Size.	Obverse.	Reverse.
			Hadrian.	
26		Æ 1·05	[ΑΥΤ ΚΑΙ]C ΤΡΑΙ ΑΔΡΙΑ[ΝΟC CЄΒ] Bust of Hadrian r., laur.	ΚΟΙΝ[ΟΝ] ΚΡΗΤωΝ Diktynna huntress, as on no. 21 (without peplos ?).
27		Æ ·85	[ΑΥΤ ?]ΚΑΙCΤ[ΡΑ ΑΔΡΙΑΝΟC]CЄΒΑC Similar.	ΚΟΙΝΟΝ ΚΡΗΤωΝ Zeus, wearing himation over lower limbs, seated l. on throne with back; holding in r. patera, in l., long sceptre; at his feet, eagle.
28		Æ ·7	[Α]ΥΚΑΙΤΡΑΙ[ΑΝΟC CЄΒΑ] Similar bust, radiate.	ΚΟΙΝΟΝ ΚΡΗΤΩΝ Nymph Amaltheia (?) r., holding infant Zeus.
29		Æ ·75	(Inscr. obscure). Bust of Hadrian r., laur.	Κ Κ (in exergue). Basket containing poppy-head and two ears of corn; on each side, torch. [Pl. I. 10.]
30		Æ ·7	ΑΥΤΟΚ ΑΔΡΙΑΝΟC Bust of Hadrian r., laur.	Κ Κ Altar, flaming, bound with wreath. [Pl. I. 12.]
31		Æ ·65	Similar.	Similar, on stand. [Pl. I. 13.]
32		Æ ·65	Similar.	Similar; altar varied.
33		Æ ·65	Similar.	Similar; altar varied. [Pl. I. 14.]
34		Æ ·65	Similar.	Κ Κ Tripod, flaming.
35		Æ ·65	Similar.	Similar.

No.	Wt.	Metal. Size.	Obverse.	Reverse.
			Antoninus Pius.	
36		Æ ·65	AYANT[Ω]NЄINOC Bust of Antoninus Pius r., laur.	K K Flaming altar, garlanded, on stand.
37		Æ ·6	Similar.	K K Altar, on which raven r. and serpent (?). [Pl. I. 15.]

No.	Wt.	Metal. Size.	Obverse.	Reverse.

ALLARIA.

End of third century B.C.—67 B.C.

SILVER.

No.	Wt.	Metal. Size.	Obverse.	Reverse.
1	235·3	Æ 1·15	Head of Pallas r., wearing crested Corinthian helmet: border of dots.	Λ Α Bearded Herakles, naked, seated l. on rock, covered with lion's skin; his outstretched r. rests on his club, his l. on rock. [Pl. II. 1.]
2	73·8	Æ ·85	Similar type: no border.	[Ͷ]ΑΤΩΙϤΑΛΛΑ Bearded Herakles, standing naked, facing; his outstretched r. rests on his club; from his l. arm hangs lion's skin. [Pl. II. 2.]
3	56·7	Æ ·85	Similar.	ΑΛΛΑΡΙΩΤΑΝ Similar: border of dots.

(Worn, and pierced.)

No.	Wt.	Metal. Size.	Obverse.	Reverse.

APTERA.

B.C. 400—300.

SILVER.

No.	Wt.	Metal. Size.	Obverse.	Reverse.
1	174·6	Æ ·95	[A] Γ ΤΑΡΑΙΩΝ Head of Artemis of Aptera r.; wearing ear-ring, necklace, and stephane ornamented with floral pattern; hair rolled. In front of head, in small letters, artist's name ΓΥΘ[ΟΔΩΡΟΥ].	ΓΤΟΛΙ ΟΙ ΚΟΣ Warrior (Apteros or Pteras), standing l. (wearing cuirass?), holding in l. spear, and shield ornamented with star; his r. hand is raised to salute a sacred tree, standing before him. [Pl. II. 3.]
2	171·8	Æ ·95	ΑΓΤΕΡΑΙΩΝ Similar, but without artist's signature: countermarked with caduceus.	ΓΤΟΛΙΟΙΚΟΣ Naked warrior (Apteros or Pteras), standing l.; holding in l. shield ornamented with star; his r. hand is raised to salute a sacred tree, standing before him. [Pl. II. 4.]
3	168·3	Æ ·9	ΑΓΤΕΡΑΙΩΝ Head of Artemis of Aptera r., wearing earring, necklace, and stephane ornamented with floral pattern; hair rolled.	ΓΤΟΛΙΟΙΚΟΣ Warrior (Apteros or Pteras), standing l., wearing helmet, sword, and cuirass, and holding in l. spear, and shield ornamented with star; his r. hand is raised to salute a sacred tree, standing before him; in field l., Ά. [Pl. II. 5.]
4	38·	Æ ·65	Head of Artemis of Aptera r.; hair rolled.	ΑΓΤ ΑΡΑ Strung bow. [Pl. II. 6.]
			(Restruck?).	
5	36·7	Æ ·6	Similar type.	ΑΓΤ ΑΡΑ Similar.
			(Restruck?).	

No.	Wt.	Metal. Size.	Obverse.	Reverse.
			BRONZE.	
6		Æ ·5	Head of Artemis of Aptera r., wearing earring and necklace; hair rolled.	ΑΠΤ ΑΡΑ Strung bow. [Pl. II. 7.]
7		Æ ·5	Similar.	Similar.
			B.C. 200—67. SILVER.	
8	35·2	AR ·65	Head of Artemis of Aptera r., wearing stephane; hair rolled: border of dots.	[ΑΠΤΑ]ΡΑΙΩΝ Helmeted warrior (Apteros or Pteras), holding in r., spear, on l. arm, round shield; moves l.; in field l., ΝΙ ΚΑ border of dots. [Pl. II. 8.]
			[A part of this coin has been broken off.]	
9	42·5	AR ·65	Head of Artemis of Aptera r.; hair rolled, and bound with cord: border of dots.	ΑΠΤ ΑΡΑ ΙΩΝ Apollo seated l. on rock; holding in outstretched r. hand, patera, and resting left elbow on lyre, which stands on the ground. [Pl. II. 9.]
10	40·	AR ·65	Head of bearded Zeus r., laur.: border of dots.	ΑΠ ΤΑΡΑΙΩΝ Hermes l., wearing petasus and chlamys over left arm; he holds in r., caduceus. [Pl. II. 11.]

No.	Wt.	Metal. Size.	Obverse.	Reverse.
			BRONZE.	
11		Æ ·65	Head of Apollo(?), laur. r.	ΑΠΤΑ ΡΑΙΩΝ Naked warrior (Apte or Pteras), facing. wears helmet, and holds in spear, in l., shield. [Pl. II. 10.]
12		Æ ·75	Head of Artemis of Aptera l., wearing stephane.	ΑΓΤΑ ΡΑΙΩΝ Race-torch. [Pl. III. 3.]
13		Æ ·6	Similar, head r.	(Inscription illegible). Similar ty [Pl. III. 1.]
14		Æ ·45	Similar.	Α ΓΤ Α Ρ Α Similar.
15		Æ ·5	Head of Artemis of Aptera r., wearing stephanos.	[Α] Π Τ (?) Three race-torch their handles crossed. [Pl. III. 4.]
16		Æ ·55	Head of Artemis of Aptera r.; hair bound with cord.	ΑΠ ΤΑ Ρ Α[Ι] Ω Ν Bee. [Pl. III. 5.]
17		Æ ·45	Head of Artemis of Aptera r., wearing stephanos: border of dots.	Α Π Lyre. [Pl. III. 2.]
18		Æ ·45	Head of Artemis of Aptera r., hair rolled: border of dots.	ΑΠ Τ Α ΙΑϘ Dove flying r. [Pl. III. 6.]

No.	Wt.	Metal. Size.	Obverse.	Reverse.
19		Æ ·55	Head of Artemis of Aptera r., wearing stephanos.	ΑΠΤΑ[ΡΑΙ]ΩΝ Warrior (Apteros or Pteras) advancing l., carrying spear and round shield.
20		Æ ·6	Similar, head r.	Α Π Τ Α Ρ Α[Ι] ΩΝ Similar type, varied.
21		Æ ·6	Similar.	Similar.
22		Æ ·55	Similar.	Similar.

ARCADIA.

Circ. B.C. 330—280.

SILVER.

No.	Wt.	Metal. Size.	Obverse.	Reverse.
1	76·3	Æ ·7	Head of Zeus Ammon r.	ΑΡΚΑ ΔΩΝ Pallas l., wea helmet, talaric chiton and loidion; head turned back; holds in r. spear; her l. rests shield. [Pl. III. 7.]
2	78·	Æ ·65	Similar.	Similar. [Pl. III. 8.]

ARSINOE.

Third century B.C.

BRONZE.

No.	Wt.	Metal. Size.	Obverse.	Reverse.
1		Æ ·8	Female head r.; hair tied in knot behind.	ΑΣ / ΡΙ Helmeted male figure, naked, r.; his r. hand raised and resting on spear, round which is coiled a serpent; his l. resting on shield. [Pl. III. 9]
2		Æ ·75	Similar.	Similar.
3		Æ ·75	Similar.	ΑΣΙ / Ρ Similar.
4		Æ ·6	Similar.	ΑΡΣΙ Similar. [Pl. III. 11.]
5		Æ ·6	Head of Pallas r., in Corinthian helmet.	ΑΡΣΙ Two dolphins, swimming l. and r.
6		Æ ·4	Head of Pallas l., in Corinthian helmet. (Barbarous).	ΑΡΣΙ Two dolphins swimming r., the lower inverted. [Pl. III. 10.]

No.	Wt.	Metal. Size.	Obverse.	Reverse.
			AXUS.	
			SILVER.	
			B.C. 350—300.	
1	10·	AR ·55	Head of Apollo r., laur.	FAΞ IΩN Tripod. [Pl. III. 15.]
			B.C. 300—67.	
2	30·2	AR ·6	Head of Zeus r., laur.	F A Tripod, above which, thunderbolt; over thunderbolt, KPA: border of dots. [Pl. III. 12.]
			BRONZE.	
3		Æ ·75	Head of Zeus r., laur.: border of dots.	ϹAΞI ΩN Tripod; in field r., [monogram]; beneath, [monogram]: border of dots. [Pl. III. 13.]
4		Æ ·75	Similar.	Similar.
5		Æ ·85	Similar.	Similar.
6		Æ ·8	Similar (countermarked with head of Apollo r., laur., and having quiver behind neck).	Similar.
7		Æ ·75	Similar (same countermark).	Similar (type and legend nearly obliterated). [Pl. III. 14.]

No.	Wt.	Metal. Size.	Obverse.	Reverse.
8		Æ ·6	Head of Zeus r., laur.	ΣΑΞΙ ΩΝ Tripod : border of dots. [Pl. III. 16.]
9		Æ ·5	Head of Zeus r., laur. : border of dots.	Σ Α Ξ Ι Ω Ν Tripod; above, thunderbolt. [Pl. III. 17.]
10		Æ ·5	Similar.	Similar.
11		Æ ·45	Similar.	[Σ] Α [Ξ] Ι [Ω] Ν Similar.
12		Æ ·75	Head of Zeus r., laur. [border of dots].	Α Ξ Winged thunderbolt : border of dots. [Pl. III. 18.]
13		Æ ·7	Similar (barbarous style).	Similar.
14		Æ ·7	Similar.	Similar.
15		Æ ·7	Similar (countermarked with head of Zeus r., laur.).	Similar. [Pl. III. 19.]
16		Æ ·7	Similar (without countermark).	Similar (countermarked with youthful head r., Apollo ?).

No.	Wt.	Metal. Size.	Obverse.	Reverse.
			CHERSONESUS.	
			B.C. 370—300.	
			SILVER.	
1	170·	AR 1·	Head of Artemis Britomartis r., wearing earring and necklace; her hair tied in knot behind and wreathed with laurel: border of dots.	ΧΕΡΣΟΝΑΣΙ[ΟΝ] Apollo, naked, seated r. on netted omphalos; holding in r., plectrum, and with l. supporting lyre, which rests upon his knee; in field r., thymiaterion. [Pl. IV. 1.]
2	167·	AR 1·	Similar.	ΧΕΡΣΟΝ ΑΣ ΙΟ[Ν] Similar, but without symbol. (Double-struck.)
3	164·2	AR ·95	Head of Artemis Britomartis l., laur., wearing earring.	ΧΕΡΣΟΝΑΣ ΙΩΝ Herakles striking l. with club held in r. hand; round his left arm, lion's skin. [Pl. IV. 2.]
4	174·	AR ·95	Head of Artemis Britomartis l., wearing earring.	Similar.
5	165·5	AR 1·05	Similar.	ΟΣΡΕΧ Similar. [Pl. IV. 3.]
6	169·2	AR ·95	Similar.	ΟΡΣΧ (*sic*) Similar.
			B.C. 300—220.	
			BRONZE.	
7		Æ ·7	Head of Pallas r., wearing crested Corinthian helmet, adorned with serpent.	ΧΕΡ Prow l.: border of dots. [Pl. IV. 4.]

No.	Wt.	Metal. Size.	Obverse.	Reverse.
8		Æ ·65	Head of Pallas r., wearing crested Corinthian helmet, adorned with serpent. (Barbarous).	XEP Prow r.
9		Æ ·65	Similar head l.	XE Similar type: border of dots.
10		Æ ·6	Similar.	XEP Similar type; above prow, X: border of dots. [Pl. IV. 5.]
11		Æ ·45	Similar head r.	XE Prow r.: border of dots.
12		Æ ·6	♀	Eagle l., wings open. [Pl. IV. 6.]
13		Æ ·65	Similar.	Similar.

No.	Wt.	Metal. Size.	Obverse.	Reverse.
			CNOSSUS.	
			Circ. B.C. 500—431.	
			SILVER.	
1	184·8	AR ·8	Minotaur, head facing, running r.; he holds in r., round stone; his l. is raised.	Labyrinth of maeander patterr centre of which ⁘; in cac the four angles is an incuse sq with a knob in the centre: whole in incuse square. [Pl. IV. 7.]
2	174·7	AR 1·1	Similar type; head l.: border of dots.	Within a square frame of the ma der pattern (Labyrinth), you male head r., with short hair b by taenia (Theseus ?): the w in incuse square. [Pl. IV. 8.]
3	186·6	AR ·9	Similar type, head facing.	Square Labyrinth formed of ma der pattern. [Pl. IV. 9.]
			B.C. 431—350.	
			SILVER.	
4	167·8	AR ·9	Head of Demeter or Persephone r., wearing earring and necklace; hair rolled and bound with corn-wreath. (Countermarked.)	Labyrinth of maeander patter centre, ⁚⁚ [Pl. IV. 10.]
5	169·	AR ·9	Similar (no countermark).	Similar; in centre, star. [Pl. IV. 11.]

No.	Wt.	Metal. Size.	Obverse.	Reverse.
6	180·2	AR ·95	Similar (countermarked).	Labyrinth of maeander pattern; in centre, star.
7	160·6	AR ·9	Similar.	Similar; in centre, crescent. [Pl. IV. 12.]
8	156·9	AR 1·05	Similar (countermarked).	Similar; in centre, star; outside each limb of Labyrinth, crescent. [Pl. IV. 13.]
9	164·1	AR ·9	Head of Demeter or Persephone l. (barbarous).	Similar; in each angle of Labyrinth, small incuse square.
10	180·4	AR ·9	Head of Demeter or Persephone l., wearing earring and necklace; hair rolled and bound with corn-wreath.	ΚΝΩΣΙ[Ο]Ν (retrograde) Bull's head, facing; to l., star (?): the whole within frame of maeander pattern. [Pl. V. 1.]
11	171·4	AR 1·	Female head r., wearing earring and necklace; hair rolled, with tresses falling.	ϘΙΒ Square Labyrinth. [Pl. V. 2.]
12	166·2	AR ·95	Similar.	Β Ι Ρ Similar. [Pl. V. 3.]
13	160·9	AR ·9	Similar.	ΒΡΙΩ[Ν?] Similar.

No.	Wt.	Metal. Size.	Obverse.	Reverse.
			BRONZE.	
14		Æ ·8	Female head l. (Demeter or Persephone ?); countermarked with square Labyrinth.	Labyrinth of maeander pattern. [Pl. v. 4.]
			[Perhaps originally plated.]	
15		Æ ·6	Head of Demeter or Persephone r., wearing corn-wreath.	Head of Zeus r. [Pl. v. 5.]
16		Æ ·55	Female head r., wearing necklace; hair rolled, tresses falling.	ΚΝΩ Head of Zeus r. [Pl. v. 6.]
17		Æ ·5	Similar.	Similar head r.
18		Æ ·4	Female head r., hair rolled.	Female head r.; hair rolled, tre falling.
19		Æ ·55	ΚΝΩ Female head r., hair rolled, tresses falling: border of dots.	Female head r., wearing earring necklace; hair rolled. [Pl. v. 7.]
20		Æ ·45	Female head r., hair rolled.	Female head r.; hair rolled. [Pl. v. 8.]
21		Æ ·6	Head of Apollo r., laur.	Labyrinth of maeander pattern; centre, star. [Pl. v. 9.]
22		Æ ·45	Similar.	Star of eight rays within do linear square. [Pl. v. 10.]
23		Æ ·45	Similar.	Similar (single linear square).

No.	Wt.	Metal. Size.	Obverse.	Reverse.
			B.C. 350—220.	
			SILVER.	
24	172·4	Æ ·9	Head of Hera l., wearing stephanos with floral ornaments, earring and necklace; hair flowing.	ΚΝΩΣΙΩΝ Square Labyrinth; in field l., arrow-head, above which, Α; in field r., thunderbolt, above which, Ρ: border of dots. [Pl. v. 11.]
25	171·1	Æ ·85	Similar.	Similar.
26	84·3	Æ ·7	Similar.	ΚΝΩΣΙ Similar; in field l. and r., Α Ρ [Pl. v. 12.]
27	83·4	Æ ·8	Similar.	Similar.
28	75·2	Æ ·8	Head of Apollo l., laur.: border of dots.	ΚΝΩΣΙΩΝ Beardless male figure (youthful Zeus?), having drapery over knees, and his hair bound with taenia (?), seated l. on square Labyrinth; he holds in outstretched r., Nike, his l. rests upon sceptre; in field l., obscure monogram: border of dots. [Pl. v. 14.]
29	34·7	Æ ·6	Similar.	ΚΝΩ Square Labyrinth; in field l., ΑΓΕ[Ι?]; in field r., thunderbolt: border of dots. [Pl. v. 13.]
30	44·8	Æ ·6	Head of Pallas l., wearing crested helmet: border of dots.	ΝΩ Ι Square Labyrinth. [Pl. v. 16.]

No.	Wt.	Metal. Size.	Obverse.	Reverse.
			BRONZE.	
31		Æ ·55	Head of Apollo l., laur.: border of dots.	[K]ИΩ (?) Square Labyrinth. [Pl. v. 15.]
32		Æ ·4	Star of eight rays; between points, pellets.	Square Labyrinth.
33		Æ ·4	Similar.	Similar. [Pl. v. 17.]
34		Æ ·45	Star of sixteen rays.	Square Labyrinth. [Pl. v. 18.]
			Circ. B.C. 220. (Alliance between Cnossus and Gortyna).	
35		Æ ·75	Bull advancing l., carrying Europa with her veil flying as a sail; beneath, dolphin l.	KNΩ (?) Square Labyrinth. [Pl. vi. 1.]
36		Æ ·7	Similar type; beneath, two dolphins: border of rays.	K N Ω ΣI ΩN Square Labyrinth; between the K and N of the inscription, star: border of dots. [Pl. vi. 3.]
37		Æ ·7	Similar.	Similar.
38		Æ ·6	Similar.	Similar. [Pl. vi. 2.]
39		Æ ·6	Similar.	K N Ω ΣIΩ N (with star). Similar.

No.	Wt.	Metal. Size.	Obverse.	Reverse.
			Circ. B.C. 200—B.C. 67.	
			SILVER.	
40	254·3	AR 1·15	Head of Pallas r., wearing crested helmet adorned with Pegasos, and foreparts of four horses: border of dots.	K NΩ ΣI Ω N Owl standing on prostrate amphora, marked with A (?); in field r., square Labyrinth: the whole in olive-wreath. [Pl. VI. 4.]
41	226·8	AR 1·1	ΠΟΛ ΧΟΣ Head of Apollo l., laur.	KNΩ Σ I ΩN Labyrinth of circular form. [Pl. VI. 5.]
42	257·7	AR 1·15	Bearded male head r., wearing diadem (Zeus or Minos); beneath, A.	KNΩ Σ I Ω N Square Labyrinth. [Pl. VI. 6.]
			(Restruck.)	
43	251·6	AR 1·15	Similar type, no letter: border of dots.	Similar.
			(Restruck.)	
44	224·5	AR 1·2	Similar type l.: border of dots.	[K]NΩ Σ I ΩN Similar.
			[Restruck on a tetradrachm of a Seleucid king.]	
45	81·5	AR ·8	Bust of Zeus Ammon l.: border of dots.	KNΩ Σ I ΩN Square Labyrinth. [Pl. VI. 9.]

No.	Wt.	Metal. Size.	Obverse.	Reverse.
			BRONZE.	
46		Æ ·9	Head of Zeus r., laur.: border of dots.	ΚΝΩ Σ Ι ΩΝ Square Labyrinth.
47		Æ ·95	Similar head l.	Inscr. obscure. Similar.
48		Æ ·85	Head of Zeus r., laur.; hair long. (Rude style).	ΚΝΩ Σ[Ι ΩΝ ?] Similar.
49		Æ ·55	Bearded male head r. (Zeus or Minos); hair bound with taenia: border of dots.	[ΚΝΩ] Σ [Ι] ΩΝ Similar. [Pl. VI. 7.]
50		Æ ·65	Similar (rude style).	ΚΝΩ ΣΙ ΩΝ Similar. [Pl. VI. 8.]
51		Æ 1·	Head of Zeus r., laur.	ΑΡΙΣ[Τ]ΙΩΝ Eagle with wings open, standing r.
52		Æ 1·1	Similar; behind head, **B**: border of dots.	[ΘΑ ?] Ρ Σ[Υ] Δ ΙΚ Α Σ Similar: border of dots.
53		Æ 1·05	Head of Zeus r., laur.; in front, half thunderbolt; beneath, **A**: border of dots.	Κ Υ Δ Α Σ Eagle with wings open, standing r.: border of dots.
54		Æ 1·05	Similar.	Κ Υ ΔΑ Σ Similar.
55		Æ 1·	Similar; beneath, **B**.	Κ [Υ] Δ Α Σ Similar.

No.	Wt.	Metal. Size.	Obverse.	Reverse.
56		Æ 1·05	Similar; beneath, Γ.	[Κ Υ] Δ Α Σ Similar.
57		Æ 1·05	Similar type; no letter beneath bust.	Κ Υ Δ Α Σ Similar. [Pl. vi. 10.]
58		Æ 1·05	Similar.	Κ Υ [Δ] Α Σ Similar.
59		Æ 1·05	Similar.	Κ Υ Δ Α [Σ] Similar.
60		Æ 1·	Similar; countermarked with [illegible] (?).	Κ Υ Δ[Α Σ] Similar.
61		Æ 1·05	Κ ΝΩ ΣΙ ΩΝ Head of Zeus r., laur.; beneath, Α; in front, half thunderbolt and aplustre: border of dots.	ΜΝΗ Σ Ι ΘΕ Ο Σ Eagle with spread wings, standing r.; beneath, Β: border of dots.
62		Æ 1·05	Similar; no letter visible.	Similar.
63		Æ ·95	Head of Zeus r., laur.; before it, half-thunderbolt; beneath, Α.	Τ ΑΥ [Ρ] [Ι] [Α] Δ [Α] Inscr. obscure. Eagle with spread wings, standing r.; between eagle's legs, letter.
64		Æ ·95	Similar; letter not visible: border of dots.	[Τ] Α[Υ] [Ι]Α ΔΑ Similar type; between eagle's legs, Α.
65		Æ 1·05	Similar head.	[Κ] ΝΩΣ[Ι]ΩΝ Similar type.
66		Æ ·85	Head of Artemis r.; on shoulder, quiver.	ΘΑ Ρ ΣΥ ΔΙ Κ ΑΣ Quiver with strap; beneath, Α. [Pl. vi. 11.]

No.	Wt.	Metal. Size.	Obverse.	Reverse.
67		Æ ·85	Similar (quiver not visible); in front, Α: border of dots.	Τ Α Υ ΡΙ Α Δ Α Quiver with strap; beneath, Α.
68		Æ ·85	Head of Artemis r., quiver on shoulder: border of dots.	Κ Ν[Ω] ΣΙ ΩΝ Quiver with strap and bow: border of dots.
69		Æ ·75	Similar.	Κ ΝΩ ΣΙ ΩΝ Quiver with strap and bow: border of dots.
70		Æ ·6	Similar.	Κ Ν Ω ΣΙ Ω Ν Winged caduceus.
			Cnossus, a Roman Colonia.	
			BRONZE.	
71		Æ ·55	C C Plough r.	O (?) Square Labyrinth. [Pl. vi. 13.]
			M. Antonius and Octavius.	
72		Æ ·8	[C I] N C [EX DD?] Head of M. Antonius r., bare; behind, square Labyrinth: border of dots.	T· FVFIO· M· AIMI [LIO II VIR] Head of Octavius r., bare. [Pl. vi. 12.]
73		Æ ·75	Similar.	[T· F]VFIO·M· AIMILI [O] IIV IR· Similar.
			Augustus.	
74		Æ ·8	C·I N CN Head of Augustus r., bare.	C· PETRONIO [M·ANTONIO] II·VIR [EX D·D] Square Labyrinth.

No.	Wt.	Metal. Size.	Obverse.	Reverse.
75		Æ ·75	Similar.	[C·]PETRON[IO] M·ANTONIO II VIR EX·DD Similar. [Pl. vi. 14.]
76		Æ ·75	Similar.	[C· PETRONIO] M· ANTONIO II VIR [EX] DD Similar.
77		Æ ·65	Inscr. ? Head of Augustus r.	C C Plough r. : border of dots.

No.	Wt.	Metal. Size.	Obverse.	Reverse.
			CYDONIA. B.C. 400—300. SILVER.	
1	172·5	AR 1·05	Female head r. (Dionysiac nymph ?), wearing ear-ring and necklace; hair rolled and wreathed with grapes and vine-leaves; behind, [monogram] (?): border of dots.	ΚΥΔΩΝ Naked male figure (Kydon ?) l., stringing bow; before him, hound, looking up: border of dots. [Pl. VII. 1.]
			(Double-struck).	
2	165·2	AR ·85	Similar head r. (barbarous copy).	Similar, without dog (barbarous copy). [Pl. VII. 2.]
3	162·	AR ·9	Similar; with countermark (race-torch ?).	Similar.
4	182·7	AR ·95	Youthful head l., wreathed with ivy.	Similar: no border.
5	143·2	AR 1·	Similar head l. wreathed with ivy: border of dots.	ΚΥΔΩΝ Naked male figure (Kydon ?) l., stringing bow; before him, hound, looking up; in field l., race-torch. [Pl. VII. 3.]
6	137·5	AR 1·	Similar.	Similar.
7	139·9	AR ·95	Similar.	ΚΥΔΩ Ν (in exergue). Hound l., suckling infant (Kydon ?). [Pl. VII. 4.]

No.	Wt.	Metal. Size.	Obverse.	Reverse.
8	91·5	Æ ·75	Head of Dionysiac nymph? l., wearing earring; hair wreathed with ivy.	ΚΥΔΩΝ Naked male figure (Kydon?) l., stringing bow. [Pl. VII. 5.]
9	66·2	Æ ·85	Head of Pallas r., wearing helmet adorned with serpent.	ΚΥΔΩΝ (in exergue). Hound l., suckling infant (Kydon?); above hound, star. [Pl. VII. 7.]
10	20·4	Æ ·4	Youthful head r.; hair short (somewhat barbarous).	Κ; around, three crescents: border of dots. [Pl. VII. 6.]
11	14·5	Æ 45	Youthful head l., wreathed with ivy.	Similar. [Pl. VII. 8.]
12	16·	Æ ·45	Similar: border of dots.	Bucranium; around, three crescents: border of dots.
13	14·	Æ ·45	Youthful head r.: border of dots.	Similar. [Pl. VII. 9.]
14	11·4	Æ ·4	Head of Persephone? r., wreathed with corn: border of dots.	ΚΥ ΔΩ Amphora, from each handle of which hangs bunch of grapes (?): border of dots. [Pl. VII. 10.]
			BRONZE.	
15		Æ ·45	Youthful male head r., hair short.	ΚΥΔ Ω Hound seated r. [Pl. VII. 11.]

No.	Wt.	Metal. Size.	Obverse.	Reverse.
16		Æ ·45	Similar head r. (horned?).	ΚΥ ΔΩ Similar. [Pl. VII. 13.]
17		Æ ·55	Similar.	Similar. [Pl. VII. 12.]
18		Æ ·45	Similar.	Similar. [Pl. VII. 14.]
19		Æ ·45	Similar.	Similar.
20		Æ ·45	Similar.	Similar.

B.C. 200—67.

SILVER.

No.	Wt.	Metal. Size.	Obverse.	Reverse.
21	211·2	AR 1·1	ΑΙΘΩΝ Helmeted head of Pallas r.: border of dots.	Κ ΥΔ Ω ΝΙΑ Owl on prostrate amphora (on which, Α?); in field r., hound r., suckling infant (Kydon?): the whole in olive-wreath. [Double-struck]. [Pl. VII. 15.]
22	230·2	AR 1·15	Π Α Σ Ι Ω Ν Head of Artemis (Diktynna) r.; behind her neck, bow and quiver: border of dots.	ΚΥ ΔΩ ΝΙΑ ΤΑ Ν Artemis (Diktynna), wearing short chiton and endromides, facing, head l.; her r. falls by her side, her l. holds long torch; beside her, on l., hound r., looking up: the whole in wreath. [Pl. VII. 16.]

No.	Wt.	Metal. Size.	Obverse.	Reverse.
			BRONZE.	
23		Æ ·9	[ΠΑΣ]ΙΩΝ Head of Apollo r., laur: border of dots.	Κ Υ Δ Ω Star within crescent: border of dots.
24		Æ ·55	Α Π Owl r.: border of dots.	Κ Υ [Δ] Ω Star within crescent.
25		Æ ·6	Α Ρ (?) Similar.	Similar. [Pl. VII. 17.]
26		Æ ·55	Α Ρ Similar.	ΚΥ Similar.
27		Æ ·5	Α Ρ (?) Similar.	Similar.
28		Æ ·6	Youthful male head l. (wreathed with ivy?): border of dots.	ΩΔ ΥΚ Bunch of grapes, with vine-leaves. [Pl. VIII. 1.]
29		Æ ·5	Female head r., wearing stephane.	Κ Υ Δ Ω Bunch of grapes. [Pl. VIII. 2.]
30		Æ ·65	Head of young Dionysos r., wearing ivy-wreath.	Κ Υ Δ Ω Crescent.
31		Æ ·7	Similar.	Similar.
32		Æ ·6	Similar.	ΚΥ ΔΩ Similar.
33		Æ ·55	Similar.	Similar.

No.	Wt.	Metal. Size.	Obverse.	Reverse.
			Imperial Coinage.	
			Augustus.	
34		Æ ·85	[K]AIΣAP ΣOTΣYΓYA Head of Augustus r., bare.	KYΔΩN I A NAT Hound r., suckling infant (Kydon?), l.
35		Æ ·85	KAI CAP Similar.	KYΔΩN[IATAN?] Similar (infant r.).
36		Æ ·85	Similar.	KYΔΩN Similar.
			Tiberius.	
37	119·	AR ·9	TIBEPIΩ KAIΣAPI ΣEBAΣTΩ EΠI KOP ΛYΠΩ Head of Tiberius r., laur.	ΣYNKΛHTΩ KPHTEΣ KY Bearded male head of Senate r., veiled. [Pl. VIII. 3.]
			Claudius (?).	
38		Æ ·7	.... KΛA .... Head of Claudius (?) r., bare.	KYΔω[N] Hound r., suckling infant, l.
			Domitian.	
39		Æ ·75	KAICAPΔOMITIAN OC Head of Domitian r., laur.	KYΔω N Similar. [Pl. VIII. 4.]

No.	Wt.	Metal. Size.	Obverse.	Reverse.
			ELEUTHERNAE. B.C. 431—300. SILVER.	
1	173·9	Æ 1·15	Head of Apollo r.; round his head, wreath or fillet composed of dots (barbarous).	ᴎ O IAᴎ[ᴎ]Ǝ ΘΥƎΛƎ Apollo, naked, standing, facing, head l.; he holds in r., bow, in upraised l., stone: all in square of dots: the whole in incuse square. [Pl. VIII. 5.]
2	170·8	Æ ·95	Head of Apollo r., laur., hair long.	ΕΛΕΥ ΑΡ Apollo, naked, facing, head l.; he holds in outstretched r., stone, in l., bow. [Pl. VIII. 6.]
3	171·8	Æ 1·05	Head of Zeus r., laur.: border of dots.	ΕΛΕΥ ΘΕ Similar. [Pl. VIII. 7.]
4	76·5	Æ ·8	Head of Apollo r. within laurel-wreath.	ΕΛΕ Similar type in square of dots: the whole in incuse square. [Pl. VIII. 8.]
5	20·	Æ ·5	Male head r. (Apollo?). (Barbarous).	[monogram] (No type). [Pl. VIII. 9.]
6	12·7	Æ ·45	Male head r.	Apollo, naked, facing; he holds in upraised l., stone, in r., bow. [Pl. VIII. 10.]
			(Barbarous).	

No.	Wt.	Metal. Size.	Obverse.	Reverse.
			BRONZE.	
7		Æ ·65	∃ Λ (Λ obscure). Bunch of grapes: border of dots.	Apollo, naked, facing, head r.; holding in r., stone, in l., bow. [Pl. VIII. 11.]
			B.C. 300—200.	
			BRONZE.	
8		Æ ·7	Head of Apollo r., laur., within linear circle: border of dots.	Ε ΛΕΥ ΘΕΡΝΑΙΩΝ Apollo, wearing bow and quiver, seated l. on netted omphalos, before which is lyre; he holds in r., stone; in field l., monogram, indistinct (monogram?).
9		Æ ·7	Similar; no linear circle.	Ε ΛΕ ΥΘΕΡΝΑΙΩΝ Similar; in field l same mon.?
10		Æ ·75	Similar.	Similar (mon. monogram).
11		Æ ·7	Similar.	Similar.
12		Æ ·65	Head of Apollo r., laur.: border of dots.	ΕΛΕ ΥΘ ΕΡΝΑΙΩΝ Apollo seated l. on rock, holding in r., stone. [Pl. VIII. 12.]
13		Æ ·7	Head of Apollo r., laur.: border of rays.	ΕΛΕΥΘΕΡΝΑΙΩΝ Apollo, wearing bow and quiver, seated l. on netted omphalos, before which is lyre; he holds in r., stone; in field l., monogram: border of dots. [Pl. VIII. 13.]
14		Æ ·7	Similar.	Similar.

No.	Wt.	Metal. Size.	Obverse.	Reverse.
15		Æ ·7	Similar.	Ε ΛΕΥ ΘΕΡΝΑΙΩΝ Similar; monogram uncertain.
16		Æ ·7	Similar; countermarked with [monogram] (?).	Ε ΛΕ ΥΘΕΡΝΑΙΩΝ Similar; monogram uncertain.
17		Æ ·7	Similar; no countermark.	ΕΛ ΕΥΘΕΡΝΑΙΩΝ Similar.

Imperial Coinage.

SILVER.

Tiberius.

No.	Wt.	Metal. Size.	Obverse.	Reverse.
18	34·3	AR ·65	ΤΙ ΚΑΙ ϹΕΒΑϹΤΟϹ ΚΟΡ Λ Υ Head of Tiberius r., laur.	ΘΕΩ ϹΕΒΑϹΤΩ ΚΡΗΤΩΝ ΕΛΕΥΘ Head of Augustus r., radiate. [Pl. VIII. 14.]

No.	Wt.	Metal. Size.	Obverse.	Reverse.

ELYRUS.

Circ. B.C. 400—300.

SILVER.

No.	Wt.	Metal. Size.	Obverse.	Reverse.
1	79·3	Æ ·7	ΕΛ Υ ΡΙο Ν Goat's head r.; beneath, arrow-head l.: border of dots.	Bee; in field l., rose: border of dots. [Pl. VIII. 15.]
2	83·4	Æ ·85	[Ε]Λ Υ [Ρ]Ιο Ν Similar.	Similar type, without rose.

GORTYNA.

Before B.C. 431.

SILVER.

No.	Wt.	Metal. Size.	Obverse.	Reverse.
1	86·6	Æ ·65	ИVTϘ◇Λ Bull recumbent r., looking back.	....Ͻ◇T........ Lion's scalp enclosed in linear square: the whole in incuse square. [Pl. IX. 1.]
2	43·6	Æ ·5	Similar type.	Lion's scalp within incuse square. [Pl. IX. 2.]
3	179·8	Æ ·85	Europa, draped, seated on bull which advances r.; her l. hand upraised, her r. resting on bull's back: beneath bull, curved lines indicating waves?	Lion's scalp within linear frame: the whole in incuse square. [Pl. IX. 3.]
4	180·3	Æ ·9	Europa, draped, seated on bull which advances l.; her arms resting on bull: linear circle within border of dots.	Lion's scalp within frame consisting of a row of pellets between two linear squares: the whole in incuse square. [Pl. IX. 4.]
5	161·	Æ ·9	Similar (barbarous).	Lion's scalp within incuse square.

No.	Wt.	Metal. Size.	Obverse.	Reverse.
			B.C. 431—300.	
			SILVER.	
6	182·8	Æ 1·15	Europa r., wearing chiton with short sleeves and peplos over lower limbs, seated r. in tree; her r. hand rests on tree, her l. arm bent and supported by her knee.	Traces of inscription. Bull standing l., looking back; beneath, grass. [[Pl. IX. 5.
7	189·	Æ 1·15	Similar, but head of Europa turned towards front.	ИOIИVTꟼOΛ Bull r., with head turned back (foreshortened). [Pl. IX. 6.]
			[Restruck].	
8	181·4	Æ 1·	Similar.	ƧИVTꟼOΛ Bull r., looking back. [Pl. IX. 7.]
			[Restruck on coin of Cnossus with four deep square depressions].	
9	173·8	Æ 1·05	Similar.	Similar type. [Pl. IX. 8.]
			[Restruck on coin of Cyrene; on the *rev.*, bearded head of Zeus Ammon r. is visible].	
10	178·5	Æ 1·15	Similar.	Similar.
			[Restruck on similar coin of Cyrene].	
11	182·-	Æ ·1	Similar; eagle's head l. in front of trunk of tree.	Similar. [Pl. IX. 9.]
			[Restruck; on the rev., letters **K** and **B**? visible].	
12	181·4	Æ 1·1	Similar; without eagle's head.	. . . ИY . . . . Similar.
			[Restruck on coin with incuse square].	

No.	Wt.	Metal. Size.	Obverse.	Reverse.
13	180·2	Æ 1·1	Similar; arms outstretched.	Bull r., looking back, his r. hind leg raised to head.
14	181·5	Æ 1·05	Similar.	Similar.
15	175·9	Æ 1·1	Similar.	Bull l., looking back, his l. hind leg raised to head. [Pl. IX. 10.]
			[Restruck on coin of Cyrene with head of Zeus Ammon and Silphium].	
16	176·2	Æ ·85	Similar.	Bull r., looking back; r. hind leg raised to head.
17	187·9	Æ ·95	Europa, wearing chiton and peplos over lower limbs, seated r. in tree; her r. hand rests upon tree, her l. slightly raises her peplos.	Bull r., looking back. [Pl. x. 1.]
18	181·7	Æ 1·05	Similar; l. hand raised to head?	Bull advancing r.: border of dots. [Pl. x. 2.]
19	184·7	Æ 1·1	Europa, wearing chiton and peplos over lower limbs, seated l. in tree; her r. hand supports her head which is turned towards front; her l. rests on tree.	ƧOꟼV[MƧT] (τισυροι) Bull recumbent l., looking back. [Pl. x. 3.]
20	183·6	Æ 1·	ƧOꟼ V M S T Similar.	Bull advancing r., looking back. [Pl. x. 4.]
21	180·5	Æ 1·	Europa, wearing peplos over lower limbs, seated in tree r., her r. hand rests on tree, her l., bent, supports her head which is turned towards front; behind, on the tree, eagle.	MOIM VT[ꟼ]O[Ꞁ] Bull standing r., looking back. [Pl. x. 5.]

No.	Wt.	Metal. Size.	Obverse.	Reverse.
22	162·7	Æ 1·	Similar; without eagle.	Similar.
23	182·2	Æ ·95	Similar.	Similar; in front, fish (?): border of dots.
24	175·2	Æ ·95	Similar.	Similar. [Pl. x. 6.]
25	182·	Æ 1·05	Similar; but Europa wears chiton and peplos.	ИOƧИ VTꟼOΛ Similar; no symbol.
			[Restruck ?].	
26	178 8	Æ 1·05	Europa, wearing peplos over lower limbs, seated in tree r., head facing; her r. rests upon hip, with her l. she raises peplos.	Similar type; beneath, dolphin r.: border of dots.
			[Restruck ?].	
27	178·7	Æ 1·	Europa seated in (leafless) tree towards r., head facing; wearing peplos over lower limbs; her l. hand is placed on the back of eagle with outstretched wings before her; her r. raises peplos above her head.	Bull l., looking back. [Pl. x. 7.]
28	177·7	Æ 1·	Same: border of dots. (Same die).	Bull r., looking back; beneath, fish
29	180·6	Æ 1·05	Similar; Europa wears necklace.	Similar type: border of dots.
30	177·8	Æ ·9	Similar; on the l. of r. leg of Europa, bull's head l.	Similar. [Pl. x. 8.]

No.	Wt.	Metal. Size.	Obverse.	Reverse.
31	81·7	AR 1·	Female head r., wearing sphendone (Europa?).	Forepart of bull r. [Pl. x. 9.]
32	85·4	AR ·8	Similar.	Head and neck of bull r. [Pl. x. 10.]
			[Restruck].	
33	87·5	AR ·85	[Ϙ]OΛ Similar.	Similar. [Pl. x. 11.]
			[Restruck].	
34	88·2	AR ·85	Female head r.; hair rolled.	Similar.
35	87·2	AR ·8	Similar; with necklace: border of dots.	Similar.
36	83·	AR ·75	Head of Persephone or Demeter r.; hair rolled, wreathed with corn; she wears earring and necklace: border of dots.	Similar. [Pl. xi. 1.]
37	81·2	AR ·7	Similar.	Similar.
38	88·9	AR ·85	Similar type: no border.	Similar. [Pl. xi. 2.]
39	87·7	AR ·75	Female head l. (Persephone or Demeter?)	Bull's head r. [Pl. xi. 3.]
			(Barbarous).	

No.	Wt.	Metal. Size.	Obverse.	Reverse.
			B.C. 300—200.	
			SILVER.	
40	95·9	AR ·8	Europa, wearing peplos over lower limbs, seated in tree r., her head facing; behind her on tree, eagle l., looking back; her r. rests on tree, with l. she raises veil.	ΓΟΡΤΥ Bull standing l., lool back: border of dots. [Pl. XI. 4.]
			BRONZE.	
41		Æ ·7	Γ[Ο]Ρ Europa, wearing peplos over lower limbs, seated in tree r., her head facing; behind her on tree, eagle l., looking back; her r. rests on tree, with l. she raises veil: border of rays.	ΓΟΡΤΥ ΝΙ ΝΩ Europa with raised over head, se on bull which advances l.: whole in wreath. [Pl. XI. 5.]
42		Æ ·8	Similar.	Similar.
43		Æ ·7	Similar.	Similar.
44		Æ ·65	Similar.	Similar (ΝΙ).
45		Æ ·65	ΓΟ Ρ Similar.	ΓΟΡΤΥΝΙ [Ν]Ω Similar type.
46		Æ ·7	Similar.	Similar.

No.	Wt.	Metal. Size.	Obverse.	Reverse.
			B.C. 200—67.	
			SILVER.	
47	249·2	AR 1·05	Head of Pallas r., wearing crested helmet ornamented with Pegasos and foreparts of horses: border of dots.	Γ OP TY NI Ω N Owl r. on amphora; in field r., bull butting r.; above bull, arrow-head: the whole in olive-wreath. [Pl. xi. 6.]
48	235·5	AR 1·1	Bearded head of Zeus or Minos l., wearing diadem; beneath, Δ: border of dots.	ΓΟΡΤΥΝΙΩΝ ΘΙΒΟΣ Pallas l., helmeted, wearing chiton with diploïs; holding in r., wreath-bearing Nike l.; her l. rests on shield adorned with gorgon's head; before her, serpent with head erect, l.: the whole in olive-wreath. [Pl. xi. 7.]
49	60·6	AR ·8	Similar head r.	ΓΟΡΤΥΝΙΩΝ Naked male figure seated l., head facing, on rock on which is chlamys; he wears endromides; his r. hand rests upon r. knee, his l. holds bow and arrow; a quiver is slung behind his back; in field r., B: border of dots. [Pl. xi. 8.]
50	42·4	AR ·65	Similar; beneath, Γ.	Similar; two arrows in hand; chlamys over shoulders; in field r., Γ.
51	45·9	AR ·7	Similar; beneath, H.	Similar; no arrows; in field r., B.
52	47·7	AR ·7	Similar.	Similar; two arrows; in field r., Δ.

No.	Wt.	Metal. Size.	Obverse.	Reverse.
53	46·7	AR ·6	Similar; beneath, Δ.	ΓΟΡΤΥΝ ΙΩΝ Similar type: border of dots.
54	62·2	AR ·75	Similar head l.	ΓΟΡΤΥΝΙΩΝ Naked male figure advancing l., head facing; his r. placed upon shield before him; his l. holds spear; in field l., wreath: border of rays. [Pl. xi. 9.]
55	46·7	AR ·65	Similar head r.	ΓΟΡΤΥ ΝΙΩΝ Similar type; in field l., ʘ: border of rays.
56	44·	AR ·65	Similar.	Similar type: border of rays.
57	74·	AR ·8	Head of Zeus r., laur.	ΓΟΡ ΤΥΝΙΩΝ Bull galloping r., carrying Europa, with veil flying over her head; beneath, A (?): border of dots.
58	33·	AR ·7	Head of Helios, three quarter face towards r.: border of dots.	Γ Ο Eagle l., holding serpent in talons: border of rays. [Pl. xi. 10.]
			[Restruck; probably on another coin of Gortyna].	

BRONZE.

No.	Wt.	Metal. Size.	Obverse.	Reverse.
59		Æ ·95	Bearded head of Zeus or Minos r., diademed: border of dots.	ΓΟΡ ΤΥ ΝΙ ΩΝ Pallas l., helmeted and wearing chiton with diploïs; in her outstretched r., serpent; her l. resting on spear; beside her, shield: border of dots.
60		Æ ·8	Similar.	Similar. [Pl. xi. 12.]
61		Æ ·85	Similar; beneath, A (?).	Similar.

No.	Wt.	Metal. Size.	Obverse.	Reverse.
62		Æ ·65	Head of Hermes (Hermes Hedas ?) r., wearing petasos: border of dots.	ΓΟ [Ρ] ΤΥ [ΝΙ] Ω [Ν] Naked male figure advancing l., head facing; his r. placed upon shield before him; his l. holds spear: border of dots.
63		Æ ·95	Head of Artemis r., hair bound with taenia and tied in bunch behind; she wears necklace, and has bow and quiver on shoulder: border of dots.	ΓΟΡΤΥΝΙΩΝ Bull l., looking back: the whole in wreath.
64		Æ ·9	Similar.	Similar.
65		Æ ·95	Bearded head of Zeus r.: border of dots.	ΓΟΡΤΥΝΙΩΝ Bull galloping l., carrying Europa with veil flying over her head; beneath, [monogram]: border of rays.
66		Æ ·95	Similar.	Similar type: border of rays. [Pl. xi. 11.]
67		Æ ·85	Head of Apollo (Apollo Pythios ?) r., hair long: plain border.	ΓΟΡΤΥΝΙΩΝ Bull galloping l.; beneath, two dolphins downwards; in field r., [monogram]: border of rays. [Pl. xi. 14.]
68		Æ ·75	Similar.	Similar; in field r., [monogram].

No.	Wt.	Metal. Size.	Obverse.	Reverse.
69		Æ ·6	Head of Apollo r., laur.: border of dots.	ΓΟΡ ΤΥΝΙ Bull butting r. [Pl. xi. 13.]
70		Æ ·5	Similar.	ΓΟΡ ΤΥΝΙ Similar.
71		Æ ·5	Similar.	Similar.
72		Æ ·5	Similar.	Similar.
73		Æ ·5	Similar.	ΓΟΡ ΤΥ Similar.
74		Æ ·45	Similar.	ΓΟΡ Similar.
75		Æ ·45	Similar.	ΓΟΡ ΤΥΝΙ Type l.
76		Æ ·5	Bearded head of Zeus or Minos r., wearing taenia: border of dots.	ΓΟΡΤ ΥΝΙ[ΩΝ ?] Bull galloping l., carrying Europa, with veil flying over her head.
77		Æ ·5	Similar.	ΓΟΡ[Τ] ΥΝΙΩΝ Bull butting l.
78		Æ ·55	Head of Hermes r. (Hermes Hedas ?), wearing petasos.	ΓΟΡΤΥ ΝΙ (?) Bull butting l.; above, caduceus: border of dots.
79		Æ ·5	Similar.	Similar.

No.	Wt.	Metal. Size.	Obverse.	Reverse.
			Imperial Coinage.	
			Caligula and Germanicus.	
80		Æ ·85	ΓΑΙΟΝ ΚΑΙΣΑΡΑ ΓΕΡΜΑΝΙΚΟΝ ΣΕΒΑΣΤΟΝ Head of Caligula l., laur.	ΓΕΡΜΑΝΙΚΟΝ ΚΑΙΣΑΡΑ ΕΠΙ ΑΥΓΟΥΡΕΙΝΩ[ΓΟΡΤ] Bust of Germanicus r., laur.
81		Æ ·85	Similar.	Similar (ΓΟΡΤ legible). [Pl. xi. 15.]
82		Æ ·9	Similar.	Similar.
83		Æ ·85	Similar.	Similar.
			Trajan.	
84		Æ ·9	ΑΥΤ ΑΥΓ ΤΡΑΙΑΝΟϹ [ΓΕΡ ΔΑΚΙ?]. Head of Trajan l.	ΓΟΡΤΥϹ Warrior armed with helmet and shield charging l.

No.	Wt.	Metal. Size.	Obverse.	Reverse.

HIERAPYTNA.

End of Fourth century B.C.

SILVER.

No.	Wt.	Metal. Size.	Obverse.	Reverse.
1	168·	Æ 1·	Bearded head of Zeus r., laur.: border of dots.	ΙΕΡΑ Date-palm; beside it, eagle r., looking back. [Pl. XII. 1.]

Circ. B.C. 200—67.

SILVER.

No.	Wt.	Metal. Size.	Obverse.	Reverse.
2	230·2	Æ 1·3	Female head r., wearing turreted headdress.	ΙΕΡΑΠΥ ΤΝΙΩΝ ΦΑΥ ΟΣ ΑΕ Date-palm; beside it, eagle l. [Pl. XII. 4.]
3	114·2	Æ ·9	Similar type: border of dots.	ΙΕΡΑΠΥ ΑΡΙΣΤ ΑΓΟΡΑ Σ Date-palm; beside it, eagle r.: the whole in laurel-wreath. [Pl. XII. 2.]
4	114·	Æ ·95	Similar type.	ΙΕΡΑΠΥ ΑΡΙΣ ΤΑΓΟΡΑ ⅃ Similar.
5	116·	Æ ·85	Similar type: border of dots.	ΙΕΡΑΠΥΤΝ (ΙΩΝ ?) ΜΕΝΕ ΣΘΕ ΝΗΣ Similar.
6	111·1	Æ ·9 (plated)	Similar.	ΙΕΡΑΠΥ ΜΕΝΕΣΘΕ ΣΤ Similar.

No.	Wt.	Metal. Size.	Obverse.	Reverse.
7	110·5	AR ·85	Similar.	[I]ΕΡΑΠΥΤΝΙ ΩΝ ΣΑΜΑ ΓΟΡΑΣ ΜΤ Similar; eagle l. (wreath not visible).
8	107·8	AR ·95	Similar.	ΙΕΡΑΠΥ Obscure letters in field r. Similar type, but eagle r. (Barbarous). [Pl. XII. 3.]
9	57·4	AR ·65	Similar.	ΙΕΡΑΠ Υ ΙΜΕΡ ΑΙΟΣ Similar type.

HYRTACINA.

Circ. B.C. 400—300.

SILVER.

No.	Wt.	Metal. Size.	Obverse.	Reverse.
1	83·8	Æ ·8	ΥΡΤΑΚΙΝΙΩΝ Goat's head r.; behind, arrow-head: border of dots.	Bee; in field r., rose: border of d [Pl. XII. 5.]
2	85·4	Æ ·75	ΙΝΙΚΑΤΡΥ Similar.	Similar.

No.	Wt.	Metal. Size.	Obverse.	Reverse.
			ITANUS. *Fifth and fourth centuries* B.C. SILVER.	
1	180·5	AR ·95	Glaukos (?) striking downwards with an object held in r. hand, his l. hand raised (holding fish ?).	Within linear square, ornamented star: the whole in incuse square. [Pl. XII. 6.]
2	174·	AR 1·05	Similar figure r., striking downwards with trident held in r. hand, and holding in l., fish.	Within linear square, star, with pellet between each ray: the whole in incuse square. [Pl. XII. 7.]
3	177·9	AR ·95	Similar.	Within linear square, ornamented star. [Pl. XII. 8].
4	173·7	AR 1·	Glaukos (?) striking downwards with trident held in r., his l. raised.	ITA Two crested sea-monsters facing one another. [Pl. XIII. 1.]
5	175·7	AR 1·05	Similar type; the trident striking fish.	ITANION Two sea-monsters facing one another. [Pl. XIII. 2.]
6	40·5	AR ·5	Similar type.	ITA Two crested sea-monsters facing one another.
7	41·2	AR ·55	Similar type; without fish.	Within linear square, similar type: the whole in incuse square. [Pl. XIII. 3.]
8	12·3	AR ·45	Similar.	Star of fourteen rays.
9	11·1	AR ·4	Similar.	Star of eight rays.
10	12·5	AR ·4	Similar.	Similar. [Pl. XIII. 4.]

No.	Wt.	Metal. Size.	Obverse.	Reverse.
11	167·	AR ·9	Helmeted head of Pallas r.	Eagle l., looking back: the whole in incuse square. [Pl. XIII. 5.]
12	77·5	AR ·75	Helmeted head of Pallas l.	ITANIΩN Eagle l., looking back; in field r., Glaukos (?), holding in l. trident; his r. hand upraised: the whole in incuse square.
13	83·7	AR ·65	Similar.	Similar. [Pl. XIII. 6.]
14	82·8	AR ·7	Similar.	Similar.
15	37·1	AR ·55	Similar.	Similar.
16	38·7	AR ·55	Similar.	Similar.
17	41·4	AR ·6	Helmeted head of Pallas r.	ITANIΩ [N] Eagle l., looking back: the whole in incuse square.
18	40·	AR ·6	Similar.	Similar.
19	10·6	AR ·45	Helmeted head of Pallas l.	Star of eight rays. [Pl. XIII. 7.]
20	11·1	AR ·45	Similar.	Similar.
21	10·8	AR ·55	Similar.	Similar.
22	11·2	AR ·45	Similar.	Similar. [Pl. XIII. 8.]
23	10·3	AR ·45	Similar type, head r.	Similar.

LAPPA.

Circ. B.C. 200—67.

SILVER.

No.	Wt.	Metal. Size.	Obverse.	Reverse.
1	40·7	AR ·7	Head of Apollo r., laur.	ΛΑΠΠΑΙ ΣΥΛ ΚΟΣ Ω Apollo, naked, moving r., holding in r. plectrum, in l., lyre: border of dots.
2	44·9	AR ·65	Similar.	ΛΑΠΠΑΙ ΣΥΛΩ ΚΟΣ Similar. [Pl. XIII. 11.]

BRONZE.

No.	Wt.	Metal. Size.	Obverse.	Reverse.
3		Æ ·85	Head of Apollo r., laur.	ΛΑΠΠ ΑΙ ΩΝ Lyre: border of dots. [Pl. XIII. 9.]

LATUS.

B.C. 200—67.

BRONZE.

No.	Wt.	Metal. Size.	Obverse.	Reverse.
1		Æ ·55	Bust of Artemis l., wearing stephane; hair tied in knot behind: border of dots.	ΛΑΤΙΩΝ Hermes, walking r., holding in r. caduceus; he wears short chiton, chlamys, petasos, and talaria: border of dots. [Pl. XIII. 10.]

No.	Wt.	Metal. Size.	Obverse.	Reverse.
			LYTTUS. *Fifth century* B.C.—300 B.C. SILVER.	
1	177·5	AR ·95	Eagle flying r.	ΛVTTS ⊙ Ν Boar's head r. within square of dots: the whole in incuse square. [Pl. XIII. 12.]
2	184·7	AR 1·15	Eagle flying l.: two borders of dots.	ΛVTTS⊙Ν Similar. [Pl. XIII. 13.]
3	156·7	AR 1·	Similar type: border of dots.	Similar.
4	169·	AR 1·	Similar type.	TSON T V Λ Boar's head l. within two linear squares: the whole in incuse square.
5	89·4	AR ·6	Eagle standing r., wings raised.	Γ YK T SON Boar's head r. within linear square: the whole in incuse square. [Pl. XIII. 15.]
6	86·1	AR ·8	Eagle flying r.: border of dots.	ΛVTT S ⊙ Ν Boar's head r. within square of dots: the whole in incuse square. [Pl. XIII. 14.]
7	88·5	AR ·8	Eagle flying l.: border of dots.	ΛVTTS⊙Ν Similar.

No.	Wt.	Metal. Size.	Obverse.	Reverse.
8	174·6	Æ ·95	Eagle flying r., with wings raised.	ΛVT Boar's head l. within linear square: the whole in incuse square.
9	191·6	Æ 1·	Eagle flying r.	Imitation of letters. Boar's head r. within linear square: the whole in incuse square. [Pl. xiv. 1.]
			(Barbarous).	
10	174·9	Æ 1·	Eagle flying l.: border of dots.	ΛYTTI ΛO Boar's head l. within square of dots: the whole in incuse square. [Pl. xiv. 2.]
11	174·2	Æ 1·	Similar.	ΛYT TION Similar.
12	179·8	Æ 1·	Similar.	ΛVTTI ON Similar type r.
13	164·5	Æ 1·05	Similar.	ΛYTTION Similar.
14	169·6	Æ 1·05	Similar.	ION ΛYTT Similar.
15	73·7	Æ ·8	Similar.	YΛT Similar.
16	78·8	Æ ·7	Eagle flying l.	Boar's head and left fore-leg l. within square of dots, outside which is a linear square: the whole in incuse square. [Pl. xiv. 3.]

Wt.	Metal. Size.	Obverse.	Reverse.
45·	AR ·65	Eagle flying l. : border of dots.	ΛΟΙΤΥΛ Boar's head r. within square of dots : the whole in incuse square. [Pl. xiv. 5.]
41·7	AR ·65	Similar.	Similar. (Double-struck).
35·8	AR ·6	Similar.	ΛVT Similar.

B.C. 300—220.

SILVER.

Wt.	Metal. Size.	Obverse.	Reverse.
54·3	AR ·7	Boar's head r. : border of dots.	ΛΥΤΤΙ ΩΝ . Eagle standing r., wings open. [Pl. xiv 6.]

BRONZE.

Wt.	Metal. Size.	Obverse.	Reverse.
	Æ ·5	Helmeted head of Athena r.	ΛΥΤ Prow r.
	Æ ·5	Similar.	Similar. [Pl. xiv. 4.]
	Æ ·7	Head of Zeus r., laur. ; in field r., Ê : border of dots.	ΛΥΤΤΙ ΩΝ Eagle standing r., wings open ; in field r., boar's head r. ; between eagle's legs, Ê : border of dots.
	Æ ·7	Similar.	Similar.
	Æ ·65	Similar.	Similar. [Pl. xiv. 7.]

No.	Wt.	Metal. Size.	Obverse.	Reverse.
26		Æ ·55	Head of Zeus r., laur.: border of dots.	ΛΥΤ Eagle standing r., wi open.
27		Æ ·6	ΛΥΤΤΙΩ Ν Eagle standing r., wings open; in field r., [monogram].	Boar's head r.: border of dots.
28		Æ ·55	ΛΥΤΤΙ Similar: mon. (?).	Similar. [Pl. XIV. 9.]
29		Æ ·55	Eagle flying r.: border of dots.	ΛΥΤ ΤΙΩΝ Boar's head l.
30		Æ ·55	Similar.	Similar. [Pl. XIV. 8.]
31		Æ ·55	Boar's head r.	ΛΥ Τ Eagle standing r.: bo of dots.
32		Æ ·45	Similar.	Similar.
33		Æ ·5	Boar's head r. within linear square: border of dots.	Similar.
34		Æ ·45	Female head r.	Eagle standing l., wings open. [Pl. XIV. 10.]

No.	Wt.	Metal. Size.	Obverse.	Reverse.

NAXOS.

Fourth century B.C.

SILVER.

No.	Wt.	Metal. Size.	Obverse.	Reverse.
1	173·2	AR ·9	Head of Apollo r., laur.	Tripod. [Pl. xiv. 11.]
			[Restruck on coin of Cnossus: traces of square Labyrinth visible on *rev.*]	
2	79·7	AR ·8	Similar.	Tripod
			(Barbarous.)	

OLUS.

B.C. 300—67.

SILVER.

No.	Wt.	Metal. Size.	Obverse.	Reverse.
1	164·1	AR 1·	Head of Britomartis l., wearing earring, necklace, and drapery on neck; her hair, tied in a bunch behind, is bound with a taenia, above which is a wreath; at her shoulder, quiver: border of dots.	ΟΛΟΝΤΙΩΝ Zeus seated l. on throne, wearing himation over lower limbs; on his outstretched r. he holds eagle; his l. rests on sceptre; in field l., [monogram]: border of dots. [Pl. xiv. 12.]

BRONZE.

No.	Wt.	Metal. Size.	Obverse.	Reverse.
2		Æ ·45	Head of Britomartis r., hair tied in bunch behind: border of dots.	ΟΛΝ Beneath, dolphin r.: the whole in incuse square. [Pl. xiv. 13.]
3		Æ ·4	Youthful head r. (Britomartis?): border of dots.	Λ Beneath, dolphin l.: border of dots.

PHAESTUS.

Before B.C. 431.

SILVER.

No.	Wt.	Metal. Size.	Obverse.	Reverse.
1	183·2	AR ·85	Europa seated on bull which advances l.; her r. resting on bull's head, her l. on his back.	A[ИM ?]ƧAƆOTΛOƧTMƧAƆ (Φαιστίων τὸ παῖμα). Lion's scalp within linear square, around which is inscr.: the whole in incuse square. [Pl. XIV. 14.]

Circ. B.C. 431—300.

SILVER.

No.	Wt.	Metal. Size.	Obverse.	Reverse.
2	172·6	AR 1·2	[O]ƧTMƧAƆ Europa, wearing chiton, and peplos over her knees, seated l. on rock, welcoming with upraised r. hand the bull advancing towards her: border of dots.	Hermes, with drapery over lower limbs, and petasos hanging at his shoulder, seated l. on trunk of a tree, and holding in his raised r. hand caduceus; his l. rests on tree. [Pl. XIV. 16.]
3	180·	AR 1·	Herakles, naked, standing facing and looking r.; he holds in r., club, in l., bow; in field l., lion's skin, in field r., barleycorn; around, four globules.	Bull's head, facing, within three-sided frame. [Pl. XIV. 15.]
4	184·8	AR 1·	Similar; without globules.	И[O]KITMI[AƆ] Bull feeding l. on grass; his l. fore-foot hobbled. [Pl. XV. 1.]

[Restruck on coin of Cnossus (?) with four deep square depressions].

No.	Wt.	Metal. Size.	Obverse.	Reverse.
5	177·8	AR ·9	Similar.	ꟽOKITMIAϽ Similar.
6	178·	AR ·95	Similar (with globules).	Within wreath, bull l., hobbled. [Pl. xv. 2.]
7	178·4	AR ·95	Herakles, naked, standing facing, holding in r. hand, club, in l., lion's skin and bow; on r., tree; above, ᑌ.	Within wreath, bull l. [Pl. xv. 3.]
8	181·	AR ·9	Similar figure; on l., serpent, on r., tree.	Within wreath, bull l., haltered and hobbled. [Pl. xv. 4.]
9	171·6	AR ·95	Similar.	Within wreath, bull r., hobbled.
10	157·	AR ·95	NOITƸIAΦ (Inscription obscure). Herakles, naked, standing facing, striking r. with club held in r. hand at serpent which springs up before him; he holds in l., bow.	Bull l. [Pl. xv. 5.]
11	181·5	AR 1·05	Herakles l., striking with club held in r. hand at Hydra which rears up before him, and whose nearest head he grasps with his l. hand; at his feet, crab; over his l. arm, lion's skin.	ΦAIΣTIΩ(?)N Bull r. [Pl. xv. 6.]
12	182·6	AR 1·05	Similar.	ΦAIΣTIΩN Similar type. [Pl. xv. 8.]

No.	Wt.	Metal. Size.	Obverse.	Reverse.
13	182·	AR ·95	ΦΑΙΣΤΙΟΝ Similar type, without crab.	Bull l. : border of dots.
14	179·4	AR 1·05	ΦΑΙΣΤΙΟΝ Youthful Herakles seated, facing, on lion's skin, holding club before him with his l. hand ; on l., bow and quiver tied to tree ; on r., vase : border of dots.	Bull walking r. : border of dots. [Pl. xv. 7.]
15	179·4	AR 1·15	Similar.	Similar.
16	175·8	AR ·95	(Inscr. ?). Similar.	Similar type within wreath.
17	183·4	AR ·95	ΦΑΙΣΣΤΙΟΝ Youthful Herakles seated, facing, on lion's skin, holding club before him with his l. hand ; in the background l., column, from which hang bow and quiver : border of dots.	Within wreath, bull butting r. [Pl. xv. 9.]
18	178·6	AR 1·	ΣΟΝΑΧΛΞΞ Zeus Velchanos, with himation over right knee, seated l. in tree ; his hair tied in bunch behind ; his l. hand rests on tree, in his r. hand he holds a cock which stands upon his knee : border of dots.	ΦΑΙΣ Bull butting r. : the whole in wreath. [Pl. xv. 10.]
19	183·1	AR 1·	Similar.	ΙΤΣΙΑΦ Bull l. : border of dots. [Pl. xv. 12.]
			[Restruck on coin of Cyrene with *obv.* Head of Zeus Ammon, bearded, l.].	

No.	Wt.	Metal. Size.	Obverse.	Reverse.
20	178·1	AR 1·	T ΑΛ ΩΝ (N) Talos winged, naked, facing and striding towards l.; he hurls stone with r. and holds another in l.	ΦΑΙΣΤΙΩΝ Bull butting r. [Pl. xv. 11]
21	86·	AR ·8	ΦΑΙΣ Youthful male head l., hair short (Herakles?) : border of dots.	Bull's head facing within wreath. [Pl. xvi. 1.]
22	48·1	AR ·55	Σ ΙΑΦ Similar.	Bull's head facing: border of dots. [Pl. xvi. 2.]
23	88·9	AR ·7	Similar type. (Barbarous).	Similar type. [Pl. xvi. 3.]
24	86·	AR ·9	Youthful male head r.; hair short. (Herakles?).	Similar.
25	43·7	AR ·6	Similar head r.	Similar. [Pl. xvi. 4.]
			[Restruck].	
26	40·4	AR ·6	Similar.	Similar. [Pl. xvi. 5.]

Third century B.C.

BRONZE.

No.	Wt.	Metal. Size.	Obverse.	Reverse.
27		Æ ·7	Talos winged, naked, running r., hurling stone with r. hand, and holding in l. another stone: border of dots.	ΦΑΙC ΤΙΩΝ Hound r. on the scent. [Pl. xvi. 6.]
28		Æ ·7	Similar.	Similar.

PHALASARNA.

B.C. 431—300.

SILVER.

No.	Wt.	Metal. Size.	Obverse.	Reverse.
1	176·8	AR 1·	Head of Artemis Diktynna r., wearing earring; hair bound with crossed cord.	Φ A Trident, with ornamented handle, upwards. [Pl. XVI. 7.]
2	172·4	AR 1·	Similar.	Similar.
3	163·4	AR 1·	Similar. (Countermarked with oval object surrounded by dots.)	Similar. [Pl. XVI. 9]
4	87·8	AR ·8	Head of Artemis Diktynna r., wearing earring and necklace; hair rolled.	Φ A Similar type: border of dots. [Pl. XVI. 8.]
			[Restruck.]	
5	86·2	AR ·85	Similar.	Similar.
			[Restruck.]	
6	41·	AR ·6	Similar.	Similar.

BRONZE.

No.	Wt.	Metal. Size.	Obverse.	Reverse.
7		Æ ·45	Dolphin r.	Φ [Pl. XVI. 10.]

No.	Wt.	Metal. Size.	Obverse.	Reverse.
			POLYRHENIUM.	
			Earlier part of fourth century B.C.	
			SILVER.	
1	41·9	AR ·65	Head of Artemis Diktynna l., wearing earring (and necklace); hair rolled: before the head in small letters, ΠΥΘΟΔ[Ω-ΡΟΥ].	Bull's head, bound with fillet: bo[r]... of dots. [Pl. XVI. 11.]
			[Restruck; probably on a coin of Argos.]	
2	37·1	AR ·65	Similar; before the head in small letters, [ΠΥΘΟ]ΔΩΡΟΥ.	Similar.
			[Restruck; probably on a coin of Argos.]	
3	39·2	AR ·65	Head of Artemis Diktynna l., wearing earring and necklace: hair in sakkos.	Similar. [Pl. XVI. 12.]
			[Restruck; probably on a coin of Argos.]	
			Circ. B.C. 330—280.	
			SILVER.	
4	163·5	AR 1·	Head of Zeus r., laur.: border of dots.	ΠΟΛΥΡΗΝΙΟΝ ΧΑΡΙΣΘΕΝΗΣ Bull's h[ead] bound [with] fillet; beneath, arrow-head, border of dots.
5	168·3	AR ·9	Similar.	Similar; in field l., caduceus.
6	176·	AR 1·05	Similar.	Similar; no symbol. [Pl. XVI. 13.]

No.	Wt.	Metal. Size.	Obverse.	Reverse.
7	166·1	AR ·9	Similar.	Similar.
8	171·5	AR 1·05	Similar type, varied.	ΓΟΛ ΥΡΗΝ ΙΟΝ Similar type. [Pl. xvi. 14.]
9	87·2	AR ·8	ΓΟ ΛΥΡΗΝΙ ΟΝ Bull's head bound with fillet.	ΓΟΛΥ ΙΝΗd Arrow-head r.: border of dots. [Pl. xvi. 15.]
			[Restruck ?]	
10	85·9	AR ·85	[ΓΟΛΥ] ΡΗΝΙ ΟΝ Similar.	Similar.
			[Restruck on coin of Cyrene; on *obv.* traces of youthful head of Ammon r., and on *rev.* part of the silphium visible.]	
11	69·6	AR ·75	ΓΟΛ ΥϤΗΝ ΙΩΝ Bull's head bound with fillet: border of dots.	ΠΟΛΥ ΡΗΝΙ Similar type.
			BRONZE.	
12		Æ ·65	Head of Pallas r. wearing crested Corinthian helmet.	ΓΟΛΥ ΡΗ ΝΙ Bull's head bound with fillet.
13		Æ ·65	Bull's head: border of dots.	Ο [Π] Υ Λ Arrow-head, upwards. [Pl. xvi. 17.]
14		Æ ·7	Bull's head.	ΠΟΛ ΥΡΗ[Ν ?] Arrow-head r.

No.	Wt.	Metal. Size.	Obverse.	Reverse.
15		Æ ·7	Round shield, in centre of which, bull's head: border of dots.	ΠΟ ΛΥ Arrow-head, upwards.
16		Æ ·5	Similar.	ΠΟΛ ΥΡΗ Arrow-head.
17		Æ ·45	Similar.	ΠΟ ΛΥ Arrow-head, upwards. [Pl. XVI. 16.]

B.C. 220—67.

SILVER.

No.	Wt.	Metal. Size.	Obverse.	Reverse.
18	239·4	AR 1·15	Male head r., with whisker; hair bound with taenia; bow and quiver at his shoulder. (Philip V. of Macedon as Apollo?).	[ΠΟ]ΛΥΡΗ ΝΙΩΝ Female figure (Artemis Diktynna ?), wearing talaric chiton, and peplos over lower limbs, seated l.; in her outstretched r. she holds winged Nike l.; her l. rests upon the seat; in ex., thunderbolt. [Pl. XVII. 1.]
19	248·7	AR 1·15	Head of Pallas r., wearing crested helmet adorned with Pegasos: border of dots.	Π Ο ΛΥ ΡΗ ΝΙ ΩΝ Owl r., on amphora; in field r., figure wearing short chiton shooting with bow r. (Artemis Diktynna?): the whole in olive-wreath. [Pl. XVII. 2.]
20	25·4	AR ·55	Bust of Artemis Diktynna three-quarter face r., draped; she wears stephane and necklace; at her shoulder, bow and quiver: border of dots.	ΠΟΛΥΡ Η ΝΙΩ Ν Youthful male figure (Apollo ?) advancing l.; his r. extended, his l. holding bow; from his l. arm hangs chlamys. [Pl XVII 3.]

No.	Wt.	Metal. Size.	Obverse.	Reverse.
21	27·5	AR ·65	Similar.	Similar.
22	27·8	AR ·6	Similar.	Similar.
			Imperial Coinage.	
			Caligula and Germanicus.	
23		Æ ·8	[ΓΑΙΟΝ ΚΑΙΣΑΡ]Α ΓΕΡΜΑΝΙΚΟΝ ΣΕ-ΒΑΣΤ[ΟΝ] Head of Caligula l., laur.	[ΓΕΡΜΑΝΙΚΟΝ ΚΑΙΣΑΡ]Α ΕΠΙ ΑΥΓΟΥΡΙΝ Ω ΠΟΛ Head of Germanicus r., laur. [Pl. XVII. 4.]

No.	Wt.	Metal. Size.	Obverse.	Reverse.

PRAESUS.

Before B.C. 400.

SILVER.

No.	Wt.	Metal. Size.	Obverse.	Reverse.
1	182·5	Æ ·95	Gorgoneion.	Within linear compartment, youthful male figure (Herakles), wearing chlamys, which flies behind, kneeling r. and shooting with bow: the whole in incuse square. [Pl. XVII. 5.]
2	186·2	Æ ·9	Youthful male figure (Herakles) wearing chlamys which flies behind, kneeling r. and shooting with bow.	ΓΡΑΙΣ Within linear square, eagle (?) standing r., wings raised: the whole in incuse square. [Pl. XVII. 6.]
3	172·	Æ 1·05	Similar type.	[Without inscription ?]. Eagle (?), standing l., wings raised. [Pl. XVII. 7.]
4	175·4	Æ ·95	Similar, but chlamys hangs from each shoulder.	ΓΡΑ ΙΣΙ (?) Within linear square, eagle (?) flying, r.: the whole in incuse square.

B.C. 400—*Second century* B.C.

SILVER.

No.	Wt.	Metal. Size.	Obverse.	Reverse.
5	168·2	Æ 1·	Zeus Diktaeus, wearing himation over lower limbs, seated towards l. on throne with back; he holds in r. eagle, his l. rests on sceptre.	ΓΡΑΙ Bull butting r. [Pl. XVII. 8.]

No.	Wt.	Metal. Size.	Obverse.	Reverse.
6	166·6	AR 1·	Similar.	Forepart of goat l., looking back: border of dots. [Pl. xvii. 9.]
7	170·8	AR 1·05	Head of Apollo l., laur.; hair long.	ΓΡΑΙΣΙ Forepart of goat l., looking back; behind, arrow-head, upwards: border of dots. [Pl. xvii. 10.]
8	75·6	AR ·8	Head of Demeter or Persephone r., wreathed with corn: border of dots.	Bull's head. [Pl. xvii. 11.]
9	79·3	AR ·7	Head of Demeter or Persephone r., wreathed with corn, wearing ear-ring and necklace.	ΠΡΑΙΣΙΟ Ν Bull's head; in field l., rose. [Pl. xvii. 12.]
			[Restruck.]	
10	66·8	AR ·8	Zeus Dictaeus, wearing himation over lower limbs, seated l. on throne; he holds in r. eagle, his l. rests on sceptre.	Forepart of goat l., looking back: border of dots.
			[Restruck on a coin of Axus; on the *rev.* the letters ΙΩ and the tripod are visible.]	
11	46·9	AR ·65	Youthful male head r.; hair short: border of dots.	Bull's head: border of dots. [Pl. xviii 1.]
			[Restruck]	

No.	Wt.	Metal. Size.	Obverse.	Reverse.
12	39·3	AR ·65	Head of Apollo l., laur. (Double-struck.)	Goat's head r. within laurel-wreath. [Pl. xviii. 2.]
13	35·8	AR ·55	Head of Demeter or Persephone l. wreathed with corn.	[ΓPA?] IΣI Bee; in field l., rose. [Pl. xviii. 3.]
14	12·8	AR ·4	Youthful male head l.; hair short. (Barbarous.)	Bull's head. [Pl. xviii. 4.]
15	12·7	AR ·4	Youthful male head r., hair short. (Barbarous.)	Similar.
			BRONZE.	
16		Æ ·7	Head of Apollo r., laur.	ΠPAI CIΩN Thunderbolt; above, ꓘ. [Pl. xviii. 5.]

No.	Wt.	Metal. Size.	Obverse.	Reverse.

PRIANSUS.

B.C. 431—300.

SILVER.

No.	Wt.	Metal. Size.	Obverse.	Reverse.
1	165·9	Æ 1·1	Female figure, her hair bound with wreath, and falling in two tresses, clad in chiton, and peplos over lower limbs, seated facing on throne with back, turned towards l.; her r. hand caresses serpent, her l. rests on seat; date-palm on r.: border of dots. (Persephone, and Zeus in form of serpent?).	ΓΡΙΑΝΣΙ ΕΩΝ Poseidon wearing himation wound round left arm and lower limbs, standing l., in r. dolphin, in l. trident: border of dots. [Pl. XVIII. 6.]
2	170·2	Æ ·95	Similar.	ΓΡΙΑΝ ΣΙΕΩΝ Similar; in field l., Π: border of dots.
3	165·8	Æ 1·	Similar.	Similar; no letter in field.
4	161·9	Æ 1·	Similar figure, wearing chiton, and peplos over lower limbs and l. shoulder, seated l. on throne; her r. hand caresses serpent, her l. placed on her dress; date-palm on r.: border of dots.	ΓΡΙΑΝΣΙΕΩΝ Poseidon standing l., wearing himation wound round lower limbs, and falling over his l. arm; in his r. he holds trident: border of dots. [Pl. XVIII. 7.]
5	80·2	Æ ·8	Female head r. (Artemis?), wearing wreath, earring, and necklace; hair rolled and tied in bunch: border of dots.	ΓΡΙΑΝ ΣΙΕΩΝ Date-palm; on l., dolphin, upwards; on r., rudder: border of dots. [Pl. XVIII. 8.]

No.	Wt.	Metal. Size.	Obverse.	Reverse.
6	70·1	AR ·75	Similar.	Similar.
7	81·1	AR ·7	Similar.	ΓϘΙΑ Similar; but dolpl downwards.
8	69·8	AR ·7	Similar.	Similar.
			BRONZE.	
9		Æ ·6	Similar.	ΓΡ Ι Date-palm: border of d [Pl. XVIII. 9.]
			Third and second centuries B.C.	
			SILVER.	
10	235·1	AR 1·2	Helmeted head of Pallas r. (Pegasos r. on helmet): border of dots.	Π ΡΙ / ΑΝ ΣΙ / ΠΥ ΡΓΙ / Α Σ / Κ Λ Owl standing facing amphora; in fiel date-palm: the wl in olive-wreath. [Pl. XVIII 11.]
			BRONZE.	
11		Æ ·65	Female head r. (Artemis?), hair rolled.	ΠΡΙΑΝ Poseidon advancing striking l. with trident held r. hand; his chlamys round l. a: border of dots. [Pl. XVIII. 10.]
12		Æ ·7	Female head r. (Artemis?), wearing wreath and ear-ring; hair rolled and tied in bunch: border of rays.	ΠΡΙΑΝCΙΩΝ Date-palm; o rudder; on r. dolphin, downwa border of rays. [Pl. XVIII. 12.]

PYRANTHUS.

Circ. B.C. 200—67.

BRONZE.

No.	Wt.	Metal. Size.	Obverse.	Reverse.
1		Æ ·55	Head of Zeus l., laur.: border of dots.	[monogram] (l.) Date-palm; on r., aplustre: border of dots. [Pl. XVIII. 13.]
2		Æ ·6	Similar.	Similar. [Pl. XVIII. 14.]
3		Æ ·55	Similar.	Similar
4		Æ ·45	Youthful male head r., short hair bound with taenia.	Similar; beneath, ΣΩΤΕ. [Pl. XVIII. 15.]
5		Æ ·45	Similar.	Similar, but the monogram on r.; aplustre on l. of palm-tree [inscription beneath, not visible].

RHAUCUS.

Circ. B.C. 431—300.

SILVER.

No.	Wt.	Metal. Size.	Obverse.	Reverse.
1	172·7	AR ·85	Poseidon, naked, leading horse r., and holding in r. trident.	ꓘYAꟼ [I]OИ Head of trident: the whole in incuse square. [Pl. XIX. 1.]
2	172·8	AR ·95	Similar: border of dots.	[ꓘY]Aꟼ I O [И] Similar.
3	170·4	AR ·9	Similar; beneath l. fore-foot of horse, ship's prow? [border of dots].	YAꟼ KIOИ Head of trident. [Pl. XIX. 2.]
4	167·5	AR 1·05	Similar: border of dots.	KIOИ YAꟼ Similar.
5	157·2	AR 1·05	Poseidon, naked, leading horse r., and holding in r. trident; in field r. AI (?): border of dots.	PAY NOIꓘ Head of ornamented trident: border of dots. [Pl. XIX. 4.]

B.C. 300—166 (?).

SILVER.

No.	Wt.	Metal. Size.	Obverse.	Reverse.
6	10·9	AR ·45	Head of Demeter or Persephone l., wreathed with corn, and wearing earring: border of dots.	PAY NΩIꓘ Head of trident: border of dots. [Pl. XIX. 3.]

No.	Wt.	Metal. Size.	Obverse.	Reverse.
			BRONZE.	
7		Æ 1·2	ΡΑΥΚΙΩ Ν Horse's head r.: [border of dots].	Dolphin r.; above it, trident r.: border of dots. (Countermark; Head of Zeus Ammon (?) r.) [Pl. XIX. 5.]
8		Æ ·8	Bearded head of Poseidon r., laur.	ΡΑΥ ΚΙΩΝ Two dolphins; between them, trident. [Pl. XIX. 7.]
9		Æ ·7	Similar.	Similar (trident obliterated ?).
10		Æ ·45	ΡΑΥΚ Two dolphins r., the lower inverted: border of dots.	Ρ Α Head of ornamented trident.
11		Æ ·45	ΡΑΥ Dolphin r.: border of dots.	Head of ornamented trident. [Pl. XIX. 6.]

No.	Wt.	Metal. Size.	Obverse.	Reverse.
			RHITHYMNA.	
			B.C. 400—300.	
			SILVER.	
1	171·6	AR 1·	Head of Apollo r., laur.; hair long.	PI Apollo, naked, facing; he holds in r. stone, in l. bow. [Pl. XIX. 8.]
2	39·9	AR ·65	Helmeted head of Pallas r.	ꟼI Head of trident. [Pl. XIX. 9.]
			BRONZE.	
3		Æ ·55	Similar.	P I I Two dolphins, upwards: border of dots. [Pl. XIX. 10.]
4		Æ ·4	Similar.	I P Head of trident, downwards.
5		Æ ·45	Helmeted head of Pallas l.	P I Two dolphins. [Pl. XIX. 11.]

No.	Wt.	Metal. Size.	Obverse.	Reverse.

SYBRITA.

Fourth century B.C.

SILVER.

No.	Wt.	Metal. Size.	Obverse.	Reverse.
1	166·4	AR ·95	Youthful Dionysos riding l. on panther and holding in l. thyrsus.	[ΣYB]PITIΩN Hermes wearing chlamys standing l., tying sandal on right leg, which rests upon a rock; before him, caduceus. [Pl. XIX. 12.]
2	5·6	AR ·35	Top of caduceus.	Σ̌ in incuse square. [Pl. XIX. 14.]

B.C. 300—67.

BRONZE.

No.	Wt.	Metal. Size.	Obverse.	Reverse.
3		Æ ·5	Head of Hermes r. wearing petasos; caduceus at shoulder.	ΣYBPITIΩN Jawbone of an animal. [Pl. XIX. 13.]
4		Æ ·5	Similar.	Similar.

No.	Wt.	Metal. Size.	Obverse.	Reverse.

TYLISUS.

B.C. 400—300.

SILVER.

No.	Wt.	Metal. Size.	Obverse.	Reverse.
1	175·9	AR 1·	Head of Hera r. wearing stephanos ornamented with floral pattern, ear-ring and necklace.	ИΩIƎI ΛYT Apollo, naked, his hair falling in two long tresses, standing l., holding in r. goat's head turned r., in l. bow; in field l. arrowhead downwards. [Pl. XIX. 15.]
2	179·3	AR 1·	Same (same die).	Similar (inscr. obscure).

AEGEAN ISLANDS.

AEGEAN ISLANDS.

No.	Wt.	Metal. Size.	Obverse.	Reverse.
			AMORGOS.	
			AEGIALE.	
			Second and First centuries B.C.	
			SILVER.	
1	31·8	AR ·6	Bearded head r., laur. (Zeus or Asklepios).	AIΓI Goat-legged Pan with horns and pointed ears, seated facing, his legs crossed; he holds syrinx to his mouth with both hands; in field l., pedum (?). [Pl. xx. 1.]
			BRONZE.	
2		Æ ·7	Goat-legged Pan standing l., his r. hand raised, his l. holding pedum.	A I Cupping-vessel with ring; beneath, Δ?. [Pl. xx. 2.]
3		Æ ·6	Bearded head r., laur. (Zeus or Asklepios).	Similar (beneath, Δ ?). [Pl. xx. 3.]
4		Æ ·65	Head of Pallas r., wearing crested Corinthian helmet.	A [I] Γ [I] Owl r. [Pl. xx. 4.]

No.	Wt.	Metal. Size.	Obverse.	Reverse.
5		Æ ·45	Turreted female head r.: border of dots.	ΑΙ Γ[Ι] Lion's head, looking l. [Pl. xx. 5.]
6		Æ ·5	Similar.	Similar.
			Imperial Coinage. Julia Domna.	
7		Æ ·9	ΙΟΥΛΔΟ ΜΝΑCΕΒ Bust of Julia Domna r.	ΕΓΙΑΛΕΩΝ Demeter in quadriga r. holding in each hand a torch.
			MINOA. *Second and First centuries* B.C. BRONZE.	
8		Æ ·6	Head of bearded Dionysos r., wreathed with ivy.	Μ Ι / Ν Ω Kantharos; above, bunch of grapes. [Pl. xx. 6.]
			Imperial Coinage. Julia Maesa.	
9		Æ 1·2	ΙΟΥΛΙΑ·ΜΑ ΙCΑ·CΕ-ΒΑ· Bust of Julia Maesa r.	ΕΠΙ Τ ΦΛΑ ΕΡΓΙΝ ΟΥ ΜΙΝΟΗΤΩΝ ΑΡΧ Apollo Citharaedus wearing talaric chiton and mantle, standing r.; he holds in r., plectrum, in l., lyre. [Pl. xx. 7.]

ANAPHE.

Second and First centuries B.C.

BRONZE.

No.	Wt.	Metal. Size.	Obverse.	Reverse.
1		Æ ·65	Head of Apollo (Apollo Aigletes?), laur., full face.	A N Two-handled vase (skyphos?); above, bee r. [Pl. xx. 8.]
2		Æ ·65	Similar.	A NA Similar.
3		Æ ·65	Similar.	[A]N [A] Similar.

No.	Wt.	Metal. Size.	Obverse.	Reverse.
			ANDROS. *Third, Second and First centuries* B.C. SILVER.	
1	52·2	AR ·6	Head of young Dionysos r., his hair long and wreathed with ivy; behind, Φ: plain border.	ΑΝΔ Ρ Ι Panther walking r. [Pl. xx. 9.]
2	100 6	AR ·85	Head of young Dionysos r., his hair long and wreathed with ivy.	ΑΝΔΡ[ΙΩΝ] Youthful male figure (Dionysos?) l., wearing short chiton; his r. is extended above a tripod, his l. is placed on the top of thyrsus (?). [Pl. xx. 10.]
			BRONZE.	
3		Æ ·7	Head of young Dionysos r., his hair long, wreathed with ivy.	Α Ν Ι Δ Ρ Amphora. [Pl. xx. 12.]
4		Æ ·7	Similar.	Similar.
5		Æ ·7	Similar.	Similar (countermark, kantharos).
6		Æ ·45	Head of bearded Dionysos r., bound with ivy.	Α Ν ? Amphora. [Pl. xx. 11.]
7		Æ ·65	Head of bearded Dionysos r., bound with ivy.	Α Ν Ι Δ Ρ Kantharos. [Pl. xx. 13.]

No.	Wt.	Metal. Size.	Obverse.	Reverse.
8		Æ ·6	Similar type r.: plain border.	Similar. [Pl. xx. 16.]
9		Æ ·5	Head of youthful Dionysos r., his hair long, wreathed with ivy.	A N Δ PI Kantharos. [Pl. xx. 14.]
10		Æ ·5	Similar.	Similar.
11		Æ ·7	Head of youthful Dionysos r., his hair long, wreathed with ivy. (Countermark, kantharos).	N A I Δ P Thyrsus; in field l., bunch of grapes. [Pl. xx. 15.]
12		Æ ·75	Similar. (Same countermark).	A N I Δ P Similar.
13		Æ ·75	Similar. (Same countermark).	Similar.
14		Æ ·6	Head of youthful Dionysos r., his hair long, wreathed with ivy.	A N Δ PI Thyrsus; in field r., bunch of grapes.
15		Æ ·6	Similar.	Similar. [Pl. xx. 17.]
16		Æ ·6	Similar.	Similar.
17		Æ ·6	Similar. (Countermark, head of Silenus r.)	Similar.
18		Æ ·65	Similar (no countermark).	Similar.
19		Æ ·55	Similar.	Similar.

No.	Wt.	Metal. Size.	Obverse.	Reverse.
20		Æ ·4	Head of bearded Dionysos r., wreathed with ivy.	A N Δ PI Tripod. [Pl. xx. 18.]
21		Æ ·4	Similar.	Similar.
22		Æ ·4	Similar.	Similar.

Imperial Times.

No.	Wt.	Metal. Size.	Obverse.	Reverse.
23		Æ ·1	Head of young Dionysos r., hair long, wreathed with ivy.	A N P Δ I Apollo Citharaedus l., talaric chiton and man holding in l., lyre, in plectrum. [Pl. xx. 19.]
24		Æ ·95	Similar.	Similar.
25		Æ ·8	Dionysos, wearing long chiton, standing towards l., holding in r., kantharos, in l., thyrsus. (Countermark, [T]PAIANOC Head of Trajan r.).	[A N] Δ PI Kantharos, above whi ivy-leaf. [Pl. xx. 20.]
26		Æ ·75	Similar. (Same countermark).	Similar.

Imperial Coinage.

Geta.

No.	Wt.	Metal. Size.	Obverse.	Reverse.
27		Æ ·7	CЄΠ·[ΓЄTAC] Bust of Geta r.	A N Δ PI ω N Simulacrum of Arten of Ephesus.

No.	Wt.	Metal. Size.	Obverse.	Reverse.

CEOS.

CEOS *in genere.*

Second and First centuries B.C.

BRONZE.

No.	Wt.	Metal. Size.	Obverse.	Reverse.
1		Æ ·7	Bearded head r., laur. (Aristaeus?).	**K E I** Forepart of dog l. surrounded by rays; Sirius. [Pl. XXI. 1.]
2		Æ ·65	Similar type.	Similar. [Pl. XXI. 2.]
3		Æ ·7	Similar.	**KEI** Similar.
4		Æ ·6	Similar.	**KE I** Similar.
5		Æ ·6	Similar.	Similar type.
6		Æ ·6	Similar.	Similar.
7		Æ ·65	Similar (head l.).	**K E I Ω N** Similar type l. [Pl. XXI. 3.]
8		Æ ·7	Bearded head r. (Aristaeus?).	**K E I** Similar. [Pl. XXI. 4.]
9		Æ ·65	Similar.	**K E [I?]** Similar.
10		Æ ·55	Bearded head r. (Aristaeus?).	**K E I** Star. [Pl. XXI. 5.]
11		Æ ·55	Similar.	**K E I** Similar.

No.	Wt.	Metal. Size.	Obverse.	Reverse.
12		Æ ·5	Head of Apollo r., laur.	Forepart of dog l. surrounded by rays (Sirius). [Pl. xxi. 6.]
13		Æ ·45	Similar.	Similar type r.

CARTHAEA.

Sixth century B.C. *or earlier.*

SILVER.

No.	Wt.	Metal. Size.	Obverse.	Reverse.
14	186·2	AR ·8	Amphora.	Incuse square, divided into eight triangular compartments, more or less deeply indented.
15	184·2	AR ·8	Similar.	Similar. [Pl. xxi. 7.]
16	172·6	Æ ·75 formerly plated.	Similar	Similar incuse square.
17	182·3	AR ·9	Amphora, on r. of which, dolphin l., upwards.	Incuse square, of mill-sail pattern; alternate compartments incuse. [Pl. xxi. 8.]
18	44·3	AR ·45	Amphora.	Incuse square, divided into seven triangular compartments. [Pl. xxi. 9.]
19	15·3	AR 3	Amphora.	Incuse square divided diagonally. [Pl. xxi. 10.]

No.	Wt.	Metal. Size.	Obverse.	Reverse.
20	17·4	AR ·35	Amphora, on the l. of which, dolphin r., upwards.	Incuse square, quadripartite. [Pl. xxi. 11.]
21	13·5	AR ·35	Similar.	Similar.
22	14·7	AR ·35	Amphora, on the r. of which, dolphin l., upwards.	Similar.
23	9·5	AR ·3	Amphora.	Incuse square divided diagonally. [Pl. xxi. 12.]
24	40·	AR ·45	Bunch of grapes.	Incuse square containing five irregular triangular depressions. [Pl. xxi. 13.]
25	38·3	AR ·5	Similar.	Incuse square, quadripartite. [Pl. xxi. 14.]
26	38·7	AR ·65	Similar.	Similar.
27	37·8	AR ·5	Similar.	Similar.
28	15·6	AR ·3	Similar.	Similar. [Pl. xxi. 15.]
29	13·	AR ·35	Bunch of grapes.	Incuse square, divided diagonally. [Pl. xxi. 16.]
30	12·6	AR ·35	Bunch of grapes.	Incuse square, quadripartite.

No.	Wt.	Metal. Size.	Obverse.	Reverse.
31	10·	AR ·3	Bunch of grapes.	Similar.
32	10·4	AR ·3	Similar.	Similar. [Pl. XXI. 20.]
33	6·1	AR ·25	Similar.	Similar.
34	88·2	AR ·75	Bunch of grapes; on r., dolphin r., downwards.	Incuse square of mill-sail pattern; alternate compartments incuse. [Pl. XXI. 19.]
35	44·	AR ·5	Similar; dolphin l., upwards.	Similar.
36	15·7	AR ·4	Bunch of grapes; on l., dolphin r., upwards.	Similar. [Pl. XXI. 17.]
37	10·7	AR ·4	Bunch of grapes; on r., dolphin r., downwards.	Incuse square, quadripartite. [Pl. XXI. 18.]
38	7·7	AR ·3	Similar; dolphin l., upwards.	Plain. [Pl. XXI. 21.]
			Second and First centuries B.C.	
			BRONZE.	
39		Æ ·75	Head of Apollo r., laur.	ΚΑΡΘΑΙ Forepart of dog r., encircled by rays; Sirius.
40		Æ ·8	Similar.	ΚΑΡΘΑ Same type l.; beneath, bee; behind dog, Σ over A. [Pl. XXI. 22.]

No.	Wt.	Metal. Size.	Obverse.	Reverse.
41		Æ ·75	Similar.	Similar.
42		Æ ·75	Head of young Dionysos r., wreathed with ivy.	ΚΑΡΘΑ Bunch of grapes, on l. of which, star. [Pl. xxi. 23.]
43		Æ ·75	Similar.	Similar.
44		Æ ·65	Head of Apollo r., laur.	ΚΑΡΘΑ Forepart of dog r., encircled by rays; Sirius; beneath, bee. [Pl. xxi. 24.]
45		Æ ·65	Similar.	Similar.
46		Æ ·55	Similar.	ΚΑΡΘΑΙ Star. [Pl. xxi. 25.]

CORESSIA.

Sixth and Fifth centuries B.C.

SILVER.

No.	Wt.	Metal. Size.	Obverse.	Reverse.
47	166·4	AR ·85	ϙ Cuttle-fish.	Incuse square, divided into eight triangular compartments, more or less deeply indented.
48	179·6	AR ·9	Cuttle-fish, on r. of which, dolphin, upwards.	Similar. [Pl. xxii. 1.]
49	187·4	AR ·75	Similar.	Incuse square, divided diagonally by broad bands. [Pl. xxii. 2.]

No.	Wt.	Metal. Size.	Obverse.	Reverse.
50	90·	AR ·6	Similar.	Quadripartite incuse square. [Pl. xxii. 3.]
51	47·9	AR ·55	Cuttle-fish [on r. of which, dolphin, upwards?].	Incuse square with six depressions.
52	45·	AR ·55	ϙ Cuttle-fish, on r. of which, dolphin, upwards.	Incuse square, divided diagonally by broad bands. [Pl. xxii. 4.]
53	13·2	AR ·35	[ϙ O ?] Similar.	Quadripartite incuse square. [Pl. xxii. 5.]
54	15·7	AR ·35	Similar type (no inscription visible).	Incuse square, divided diagonally by broad bands.
55	7·4	AR ·3	ϙO Dolphin l.	Incuse square, containing four triangular depressions. [Pl. xxii. 6.]
56	5·4	AR ·3	Similar.	Plain. [Pl. xxii. 7.]
			Second and First centuries B.C.	
			BRONZE.	
57		Æ ·5	Bearded male head r. (Aristaeus?).	ΚΟΡΗ Star. [Pl. xxii. 8.]
58		Æ ·45	Similar.	Similar.
59		Æ ·55	Similar.	ΚΟΡΗ....Ο.. Star.

No.	Wt.	Metal. Size.	Obverse.	Reverse.
60		Æ ·45	Cuttle-fish, on l. of which, dolphin l., upwards.	K O Bunch of grapes. [Pl. xxii. 9.]
61		Æ ·45	Cuttle-fish.	Similar.
62		Æ ·4	Similar.	Similar. [Pl. xxii. 10.]
63		Æ ·75	Head of Apollo Smintheus r., laur.; before head, V.	K O P H Bunch of grapes; in field r., bee; in field l., V. [Pl. xxii. 11.]
64		Æ ·65	Similar type.	Similar.
65		Æ ·65	Similar.	Similar.
66		Æ ·8	Head of Apollo Smintheus r., laur.	KO PH Bee. [Pl. xxii. 12.]

IULIS.

Second and First centuries B.C.

BRONZE.

No.	Wt.	Metal. Size.	Obverse.	Reverse.
67		Æ ·5	Head of Apollo r., laur.	O Y I Bee. [Pl. xxii. 13.]
68		Æ ·55	Similar.	Similar.

No.	Wt.	Metal. Size.	Obverse.	Reverse.
69		Æ ·4	Head of bearded Dionysos r.	Ι ΟΥ Bunch of grapes. [Pl. xxii. 14.]
70		Æ ·4	Similar.	ΙΟΥ Similar.
71		Æ ·35	Head of Artemis r.	ΙΟ Υ Bee within wreath. [Pl. xxii. 15.]
72		Æ ·35	Similar.	Similar.
73		Æ ·45	Similar.	Similar.
74		Æ ·4	Similar.	Ι Ο Υ Similar.
75		Æ ·65	Head of Artemis r.	Ε ΙΟΥ ΛΙ Bunch of grapes. [Pl. xxii. 16.]
76		Æ ·6	Similar type.	Λ Ι ΙΟ Υ Similar. [Pl. xxii. 17.]
77		Æ ·6	Similar.	Similar.
78		Æ ·6	Bearded head r., laur.: border of dots.	ΙΟΥΛΙ Ε Bee. [Pl. xxii. 18.]
79		Æ ·6	Similar.	Similar.
80		Æ ·6	Similar.	Similar.

No.	Wt.	Metal. Size.	Obverse.	Reverse.
81		Æ ·5	Similar.	ΙΟΥ [ΛΙΕ] Bee.
82		Æ ·55	Similar.	[ΙΟΥΛΙ] Ε Similar.
83		Æ ·5	Similar.	Bee; in field l., ⊕ ? (inscr. not visible).
84		Æ ·45	Bee.	Star. [Pl. XXII. 19.]
85		Æ ·35	Similar.	Similar.

CYTHNOS.

Second and First centuries B.C.

BRONZE.

No.	Wt.	Metal. Size.	Obverse.	Reverse.
1		Æ ·7	Head of Apollo r., laur.	K Y Lyre. [Pl. XXII. 20.]
2		Æ ·65	Head of Apollo r., laur.: border of dots.	K Y / Θ N Lyre. [Pl. XXII. 21.]
3		Æ ·6	Head of Apollo r., laur.	K Y / ʘ N Lyre. [Pl. XXII. 22.]
4		Æ ·6	Female head r.	K Y Bunch of grapes.
5		Æ ·55	Similar.	Similar. [Pl. XXII. 23.]
6		Æ ·6	Head of Apollo r.	K Y / ʘ NI Rose. [Pl. XXII. 24.]
7		Æ ·5	Similar type; behind, K?	K Y Rose.
8		Æ ·35	Female head r. (Artemis?).	K Y Rose.
9		Æ ·35	Similar.	K Y / ʘ N Rose.
10		Æ ·35	Dog standing r.	K Y Rose. [Pl. XXII. 25.]

DELOS.

Circ. B.C. 200—B.C. 87.

BRONZE.

Wt.	Metal. Size.	Obverse.	Reverse.
	Æ ·7	Head of Apollo l., laur. ; behind, (?).	Δ H Palm-tree. [Pl. XXIII 1.]
	Æ ·45	Head of Artemis l.	Δ H Palm-tree, above which, swan l. [Pl. XXIII. 2.]
	Æ ·45	Similar type ; behind neck, quiver.	Similar.
	Æ ·65	Head of Apollo l., laur.	Δ H Lyre. [Pl. XXIII. 3.]
	Æ ·4	Head of Apollo r., laur.	Δ H Lyre. [Pl. XXIII. 4.]
	Æ ·4	Head of Apollo l., laur.	Similar.
	Æ ·4	Similar.	Similar. [Pl. XXIII. 5.]
	Æ ·4	Similar.	Similar.
	Æ ·4	Head of Apollo r., laur.	Δ [H] Lyre ; in field l., cornucopiae. [Pl. XXIII. 6.]
	Æ ·4	Similar.	Δ H Lyre ; in field r., swan l.

GYAROS.

Imperial Times?

BRONZE.

No.	Wt.	Metal. Size.	Obverse.	Reverse.
1		Æ ·5	Bust of Artemis r.; quiver at shoulder.	ΓΥΑ ΡΙΩΝ Quiver with strap. [Pl. xxiii. 7.]

No.	Wt.	Metal. Size.	Obverse.	Reverse.

IOS.

Second and First centuries B.C.

BRONZE.

No.	Wt.	Metal. Size.	Obverse.	Reverse.
1		Æ ·75	ΟΜΗΡΟΥ Bearded head of Homer r., bound with taenia. (Countermark, Head of Helios r.)	ΙΗΤ ΩΝ Pallas r., holding in l. shield, and with r. hurling spear; before her, small palm-tree. [Pl. XXIII. 8.]
2		Æ ·8	Similar. (Countermark, Uncertain head.)	Similar. (Countermark, Ι Η and a figure of Pallas similar to that forming the type.)
3		Æ ·85	Similar. (Countermark, Female head r.)	Similar; same countermark. [Pl. XXIII. 9.]
4		Æ ·6	Similar (no countermark).	Similar (no countermark). [Pl. XXIII. 10.]
5		Æ ·45	ΟΜΗΡΟΥ Bearded head of Homer r., bound with taenia.	ΙΗ ΤΩ[Ν] Palm-tree.
6		Æ ·65	ΟΜΗΡΟΥ Bearded head of Homer l., bound with taenia.	Ι ΗΤ Palm-tree. [Pl. XXIII. 11.]
7		Æ ·55	Similar; type r.	ΙΗ Τ Palm-tree.

No	Wt.	Metal. Size.	Obverse.	Reverse.
			Probably of Imperial Times.	
			BRONZE.	
8		Æ ·95	Head of Homer r., hair short, bound with taenia : border of dots.	ΙΗ ΤΩΝ Pallas r., holding in l., shield, and hurling spear with r. [Pl. xxiii. 13.]
9		Æ ·75	ΟΜΗΡΟ Υ Similar head r. : border of dots.	ΙΗ Τ ΩΝ Pallas standing l., holds in r. patera over lighted altar; in l. she holds spear ; behind her, shield : border of dots. [Pl. xxiii. 12.]
			Imperial Coinage.	
			Trajan.	
10		Æ 1·15	[Ν]ЄΡΤΡΑΙΑΝΟϹ .... Bust of Trajan r., laur., wearing paludamentum and cuirass.	[Ι]ΗΤ ΩΝ Pallas standing l., holding in r. patera, in l. spear; behind her, shield. [Pl. xxiii. 15.]
			Faustina Junior.	
11		Æ ·85	ΦΑVϹΤЄ ΙΝΑ ϹЄ-ΒΑϹ Bust of Faustina Junior r.	ΙΗΤ ΩΝ Palm-tree. [Pl. xxiii. 14.]
12		Æ ·8	ΦΑVϹΤЄΙ ΝΑϹЄΒΑ Similar.	ΙΗ ΤΩΝ Similar.

No.	Wt.	Metal. Size.	Obverse.	Reverse.
			MELOS.	
			Fourth century B.C.	
			SILVER.	
1	123·	AR ·8	Pomegranate with leaves: border of dots. (Countermark, Corinthian helmet r.)	ΜΑ ΛΙ Kantharos. [Pl. XXIII. 16.]
2	32·4	AR ·55	Pomegranate.	Youthful male figure (Herakles ?) r., naked, kneeling on right knee and shooting with bow. [Pl. XXIII. 17.]
			Fourth—First century, B.C.	
			BRONZE.	
3		Æ ·65	Pomegranate.	Youthful male figure (Herakles ?) r., naked, kneeling on right knee and shooting with bow. [Pl. XXIII. 19.]
4		Æ ·65	Pomegranate.	Bow-case (?). [Pl. XXIII. 20.]
5		Æ ·4	Pomegranate.	Type obscure (bow-case ?)
6		Æ ·5	Pomegranate.	Phrygian helmet, with cheek-pieces, l. [Pl. XXIII. 21.]
7		Æ ·4	Pomegranate.	Corinthian helmet r.

No.	Wt.	Metal. Size.	Obverse.	Reverse.
8		Æ ·4	Similar.	Similar type. [Pl. xxiii. 22.]
9		Æ ·55	Pomegranate.	Star.
10		Æ ·5	Pomegranate.	Scallop-shell. [Pl. xxiii. 23.]
11		Æ ·65	Pomegranate with leaves: border of dots.	Μ Α Kantharos with bunch of grapes hanging from each handle: the whole in incuse square. [Pl. xxiii. 18.]
12		Æ ·65	Similar.	Similar.
13		Æ ·65	Pomegranate.	Μ Α Kantharos bound with wreath and having grapes hanging from each handle; above, ivy-leaf. [Pl. xxiv. 1.]
14		Æ ·65	Similar.	Similar; no wreath or leaf above kantharos.
15		Æ ·6	Similar.	Similar.
16		Æ ·45	Pomegranate.	Μ Kantharos. [Pl. xxiv. 2.]
17		Æ ·45	Similar.	Similar type.
18		Æ ·45	Similar.	Similar. [Pl. xxiv. 3.]
19		Æ ·4	Similar.	Similar.

No.	Wt.	Metal. Size.	Obverse.	Reverse.
20		Æ ·5	Pomegranate: plain border.	Bunch of grapes.
21		Æ ·4	Similar type.	Similar.
22		Æ ·85	Pomegranate: border of dots.	Cornucopiae bound with fillet, between pilei of Dioscuri, each surmounted by star: the whole in wreath of olive. [Pl. xxiv. 4.]
23		Æ ·9	Similar.	Similar.
24		Æ ·85	Similar.	Similar.
25		Æ ·7	Similar.	Similar.
26		Æ ·85	Pomegranate.	[M] A Beardless male head r., wearing crested Corinthian helmet. [Pl. xxiv. 5.]
27		Æ ·7	Pomegranate.	Pallas r., holding in l. shield, with r. hurling spear; behind her, krater as countermark.
28		Æ ·7	Similar.	Similar figure of Pallas; before her, krater. (No countermark).
29		Æ ·6	Pomegranate: border of dots.	Amphora within compartment composed of two vertical lines joined by one horizontal line: border of dots. [Pl. xxiv. 6.]
30		Æ ·45	Pomegranate: border of dots.	Lyre: border of dots. [Pl. xxiv. 7.]
31		Æ ·45	Similar type.	Similar type.

No.	Wt.	Metal. Size.	Obverse.	Reverse.
			Roman Times, probably Imperial.	
			BRONZE.	
32		Æ ·9	**BOVΛH** Bust of Boule r., laur. and draped: border of dots.	**MHΛ I Ω N** Owl r. wi olive-wreath: border of dots. [Pl. xxiv. 8.]
33		Æ ·75	Similar.	Similar.
34		Æ ·75	Similar.	Similar.
35	183·5	Æ 1·05	**ΔPAXMH** Bust of Pallas r., wearing crested Corinthian helmet.	**MHΛI Ω N** within olive-wreath.
36		Æ 1·05	**И ΩIΛHM** Similar type: border of dots.	**MHΛ IΩN** within olive-wreath. [Pl. xxiv. 9.]
37		Æ ·9	Similar type.	**HM IΛ ИW** within olive-wreath.
38		Æ 1·	Similar type: bead and reel border.	**MH ΛIWN** within olive-wreath. [Pl. xxiv. 10.]
39		Æ ·7	Bust of Pallas r., wearing crested Corinthian helmet: border of dots.	**MHΛ...** Bull walking r.: bo of dots. [Pl. xxiv. 11.]
40		Æ ·45	Head of Pallas r., wearing crested Corinthian helmet: border of dots.	Pomegranate within wreath. [Pl. xxiv. 14.]

No.	Wt.	Metal. Size.	Obverse.	Reverse.
41		Æ ·8	Inscription ? Branch bearing three pomegranates, with stalks united.	ΜΗ ΛΙ ѠΝ within olive-wreath. [Pl. XXIV. 12.]
42		Æ ·95	ΕΠΙ·ΤΙ·ΠΑΝΚΛΕΟϹ ΤΟ·Γ Pomegranate.	ΜΗΛΙΩΝ Simulacrum of Pallas with helmeted head looking r.; in r. hand spear, in l. shield; in field r., III. [Pl. XXIV. 13.]
43		Æ 1·	[ΒΟΥΛΗ]ΜΗΛΙΩΝ Head of Boule r., veiled; beneath, Μ ?	ΕΠΙ ΤΙ·ΠΑΝ ΚΛΕΟϹ ΤΟ·Γ within olive-wreath: border of dots. [Pl. XXIV. 15.]
44		Æ ·75	ΜΗΛΙΩΝ Helmeted head of Pallas r.; behind, pomegranate.	Similar. [Pl. XXIV. 16.]
45		Æ ·7	Similar.	Similar.
46		Æ ·75	Similar.	Similar.

Imperial Coinage.

Commodus.

No.	Wt.	Metal. Size.	Obverse.	Reverse.
47		Æ ·9	ΑΥΚ ΚΟΜ ΟΔΟϹ- ΜΗΛΙΩ Ν Head of Commodus r., laur.	ЄΠΙ ΑΡΧ Φ ΛЄ·ΠΑ ΦΡΟΔΙ ΤΟΥ within olive-wreath.
48		Æ ·55	ΜΗΛΙΩΝ Helmeted head of Pallas r.	ЄΠΙ ΑΡΧ[Φ] ΛЄΠΑ ΦΡΔΙ (*sic*) [Τ]ΟΥ within olive-wreath.

No.	Wt.	Metal. Size.	Obverse.	Reverse.
			MYCONOS.	
			Third and Second centuries B.C.?	
			BRONZE.	
1		Æ ·65	Head of bearded Dionysos r.; hair long, wreathed with ivy.	M [Y] K [O] Grain of corn and bun of grapes. [Pl. xxv. 1.]
2		Æ ·65	Similar type (hair short).	Similar.
3		Æ ·7	Head of young Dionysos, three-quarter face r., wreathed with ivy.	M Y K O Grain of corn and bur of grapes. [Pl. xxv. 2.]
4		Æ ·4	Head of bearded Dionysos r.; hair long, wreathed with ivy.	M Y [K] O Grain of corn and bur of grapes.
5		Æ ·4	Female head r. (Demeter?).	M Y K O Grain of corn and bur of grapes. [Pl. xxv. 6.]
6		Æ ·4	Similar.	Similar.
			First century B.C. *and Imperial Times.*	
			BRONZE.	
7		Æ ·7	Head of young Dionysos, three-quarter face towards r., wreathed with ivy.	M Y K [O] Grain of corn and bu of grapes; in field thyrsus. [Pl. xxv. 3.]
8		Æ ·6	Similar.	M Y K O Bunch of grapes and gr of corn; in field l., th sus. [Pl. xxv. 4.]

No.	Wt.	Metal. Size.	Obverse.	Reverse.
9		Æ ·6	Similar head.	M Y K O Bunch of grapes and ear of corn; in field l., thyrsus.
10		Æ ·7	Head of young Dionysos, three-quarter face towards r., wreathed with ivy.	M Y K O NI Ω N Corn-stalk bearing two ears. [Pl. xxv. 5.]
11		Æ ·7	Similar (head larger).	Similar.

No.	Wt.	Metal. Size.	Obverse.	Reverse.
			NAXOS.	
			Sixth century B.C., *or earlier.*	
			SILVER.	
1	186·9	AR ·85	Kantharos wreathed with ivy-leaves; from each handle, bunch of grapes suspended; above, ivy-leaf.	Incuse square divided into four compartments.
2	190·5	AR ·85	Similar.	Similar. [Pl. xxv. 7.]
3	188·9	AR ·85	Similar.	Similar.
4	191·1	AR ·8	Similar (without ivy-wreath?).	Similar. [Pl. xxv. 8.]
5	18·8	AR ·4	Kantharos, above which, ivy-leaf.	Similar. [Pl. xxv. 9.]
6	17·7	AR ·4	Similar.	Similar.
			Fourth century B.C.	
			SILVER.	
7	57·5	AR ·55	Head of bearded Dionysos r., wearing ivy-wreath.	. . . ΙΩΝ Kantharos; above, ivy-leaf. [Pl. xxv. 10.]

No.	Wt.	Metal. Size.	Obverse.	Reverse.
			BRONZE.	
8		Æ ·45	Head of bearded Dionysos l., wearing ivy-wreath.	N A Kantharos; attached to each handle, ivy-leaf; above, bunch of grapes. [Pl. xxv. 11.]
9		Æ ·45	Similar.	Similar.
10		Æ ·45	Similar.	Similar.
11		Æ ·45	Similar.	Similar.
12		Æ ·45	Similar.	Similar.
			Third and Second centuries B.C.	
			BRONZE.	
13		Æ ·8	Head of young Dionysos l., wearing ivy-wreath.	N [A] Ξ [I] Krater and thyrsus. [Pl. xxv. 12.]
14		Æ ·7	Similar.	N [A] Ξ [I] Thyrsus and krater. [Pl. xxv. 13.]
15		Æ ·8	Head of young Dionysos r., wreathed with ivy.	N A Ξ I Krater between two thyrsi. [Pl. xxv. 14.]
16		Æ ·8	Similar.	Similar. (Countermark, Corinthian helmet l.)

No.	Wt.	Metal. Size.	Obverse.	Reverse.
17		Æ ·8	Head of young Dionysos r., wearing ivy-wreath.	N A Ξ I Krater and thyrsus. [Pl. xxv. 15.]
18		Æ ·65	Head of bearded Dionysos r., wearing ivy-wreath: border of dots.	N A Ξ I Kantharos; above, bunch of grapes. [Pl. xxv. 16.]
19		Æ ·6	Similar.	Similar.
20		Æ ·65	Similar.	Similar.
21		Æ ·6	Head of young Dionysos r., wearing ivy-wreath.	N A Ξ I Bunch of grapes.
			Imperial Coinage.	
			Julia Domna.	
22		Æ ·95	IOVΛIA ΔOM NA CЄBAC Bust of Julia Domna r.	NAΞ IΩN The Three Charites.
			Geta.	
23		Æ ·55	[Λ·CЄ] ΠΓЄTA[C] Head of Geta r., bare.	N[AΞI]ΩN Amphora.

No.	Wt.	Metal. Size.	Obverse.	Reverse.

PAROS.

Seventh and Sixth centuries B.C.

SILVER.

No.	Wt.	Metal. Size.	Obverse.	Reverse.
1	190·1	AR ·8	Goat r., looking back, with r. foreleg bent; beneath, dolphin r.	Incuse square divided into six compartments of triangular form. [Pl. xxvi. 1.]
2	187·7	AR ·75	Similar.	Similar.

Fourth century B.C.

SILVER.

No.	Wt.	Metal. Size.	Obverse.	Reverse.
3	29·8	AR ·5	Goat r.	ΓΑ Ear of bearded wheat. [Pl. xxvi. 2.]
4	27·8	AR ·45	Similar.	Similar.
5	28·6	AR ·5	ΓΑΡ Similar type.	Wreath composed of two corn-stalks with ears. [Pl. xxvi. 3.]

BRONZE.

No.	Wt.	Metal. Size.	Obverse.	Reverse.
6		Æ ·45	Goat r.	ΓΑ Ear of bearded wheat. [Pl. xxvi. 4.]
7		Æ ·45	Similar.	ΓΑ ΡΙ Similar.
8		Æ ·45	ΓΑ Goat r.	ΡΙ Similar.
9		Æ ·45	ΓΑ Goat l.	Similar.
10		Æ ·4	Female head r.	ΓΑ Goat r. [Pl. xxvi. 5.]

No.	Wt.	Metal. Size.	Obverse.	Reverse.
			Third century B.C.	
			SILVER.	
11	118·1	Æ ·9	Female head r. (Artemis?); hair short and tied with band passing round thrice.	ΑΝΑΞΙΚ ΓΑΡΙ Goat r. [Pl. xxvi. 6.]
12	110·4	Æ ·85	Similar.	Similar.
13	116·	Æ ·85	Head of Demeter r., veiled and wreathed with corn.	ΓΑΡΙ within ivy-wreath berries. [Pl. xxvi. 7.]
14	48·7	Æ ·7	Head of Demeter or Persephone r., with earring; hair rolled and wreathed with corn.	Similar. [Pl. xxvi. 8.]
15	52·6	Æ ·6	Similar head, with earring and necklace.	Similar; wreath varied; above i Θ. [Pl. xxvi. 9.]
			Second century B.C.	
			SILVER.	
16	240·	Æ 1·05	Head of young Dionysos r., wreathed with ivy.	ΑΡΙΣΤΟΔΗ[Μ] ΓΑΡΙΩΝ Female f (Demeter The phoros?) seated l. on cista tica, holding in r. two ea corn, in l., sceptre; she wears ton, and peplos over her l limbs; her hair is wreathed corn. [Pl. xxvi. 10.]

No.	Wt.	Metal. Size.	Obverse.	Reverse.
17	118·6	AR ·9	Female head r. (Artemis?); hair short and tied with band passing round thrice.	ΑΚΟΥ * ΠΑΡΙ Goat r. [Pl. XXVI. 11.]
18	109·1	AR ·9	Similar.	ΚΤΗΣ ΠΑΡΙ Similar.
19	86·3	Æ ·85 (plated)	Similar.	[. . Λ ?] ΠΑΡΙ Similar.
			LATER BRONZE COINAGE.	
			Third, Second and First centuries B.C.	
20		Æ ·8	Female head r. (Artemis?); hair short and tied with band passing round thrice.	ΓΑΡΙ Goat kneeling r. [Pl. XXVI. 12.]
21		Æ ·65	Head of Artemis (?) r., wearing stephane; hair rolled.	[Γ]ΑΡΙ Goat r. [Pl. XXVI. 13.]
22		Æ ·6	Similar.	Similar.
23		Æ ·45	Female head r., bound with corn-wreath (?); hair rolled.	Π Α ΡΙ Corn-stalk bearing two ears. [Pl. XXVI. 14.]
24		Æ ·4	Head of Demeter or Persephone r., bound with corn-wreath; hair rolled.	Γ Α Ρ Ι Ear of wheat.
25		Æ ·4	Similar head r.	Similar.

* The forms of the letters are later than those in nos. 11, 12.

No.	Wt.	Metal. Size.	Obverse.	Reverse.
26		Æ ·55	Head of young Dionysos r., wreathed with ivy.	ΓAP within wreath of wheat. [Pl. xxvi. 15.]
27		Æ ·7	Head of Demeter r., veiled and wreathed with corn.	ΠAPI Goat r.; before him, ear of wheat erect. [Pl. xxvi. 16.]
28		Æ ·7	Female head r., wearing stephane; hair rolled: plain border.	Π A P I Cornucopiae bound with fillet; in field l., monogram MP? [Pl. xxvi. 17.]
29		Æ ·75	Female head r. (Artemis?), hair rolled and tied with band passing round thrice.	ΠAPI Goat r.; r. foreleg bent.
30		Æ ·75	Similar.	Similar. [Pl. xxvi. 19.]
31		Æ ·75	Similar.	Similar.
32		Æ ·65	Head of Demeter or Persephone r., wreathed with corn.	ΠAPI Goat r.; in front, a star. [Pl. xxvi. 18.]
33		Æ ·65	Similar.	Similar.
34		Æ ·65	Similar.	Similar.
35		Æ ·65	Similar.	Similar; countermark, pomegranate?
36		Æ ·65	Similar.	Similar; countermark, pomegranate.

No.	Wt.	Metal. Size.	Obverse.	Reverse.
37		Æ ·65	Similar.	ΠΑ ΡΙ Same type (no countermark).
38		Æ ·6	Similar.	Similar.
			Imperial Coinage.	
			M. Aurelius.	
39		Æ 1·	Α[ΥΤ]ΑΥ[Ρ] ΑΝ-Τ[Ω]ΝΕΙΝΟϹ Bust of M. Aurelius r., laur.	ΠΑ [ΡΙΩΝ] Helmeted female bust r. (Pallas or Roma).

PHOLEGANDROS.

Second and First centuries B.C.

BRONZE.

No.	Wt.	Metal. Size.	Obverse.	Reverse.
1		Æ ·8	Youthful head r. (Apollo?).	ΦΟΛΕ Bull butting r. [Pl. XXVII. 1.]
2		Æ ·6	Similar.	Similar.

No.	Wt.	Metal. Size.	Obverse.	Reverse.
			SERIPHOS.	
			Circ. B.C. 300.	
			BRONZE.	
1		Æ ·45	Head of Perseus r., wearing winged helmet surmounted by vulture's head.	ΣEPI Harpa. [Pl. XXVII. 2.]
			Second and First centuries B.C. *and Imperial Times.*	
			BRONZE.	
2		Æ ·5	Head of Perseus r., winged and bound with taenia.	ΣE PI Perseus r. wearing winged helmet; he holds harpa and gorgon's head. [Pl. XXVII. 3.]
3		Æ ·6	Head of Perseus r., wearing winged helmet with vulture's head.	[Σ E] Gorgon's head; beneath, harpa r. [Pl. XXVII. 4.]
4		Æ ·65	Helmeted head of Perseus r.	Σ E Gorgon's head; beneath, harpa r. [Pl. XXVII. 5.]
5		Æ ·6	Similar; countermark, harpa.	Similar.
6		Æ ·7	Head of Perseus r.; countermark, thunderbolt.	[Σ]E PI Gorgon's head; beneath, harpa l.
7		Æ ·55	Head of Perseus r., wearing helmet surmounted by vulture's head.	Gorgon's head. [Pl. XXVII. 6.]
8		Æ ·55	Similar type.	[Σ]E PI Harpa, upwards.

No.	Wt.	Metal. Size.	Obverse.	Reverse.
9		Æ ·45	Head of Perseus r., wearing winged helmet surmounted by vulture's head.	ΣΕ[ΡΙ] Harpa r.
10		Æ ·6	Gorgon's head; beneath, harpa l.	[CЄPЄIΦI ?]ωN Perseus advancing l., holding in l. harpa. [Pl. xxvii. 7.]
11		Æ ·55	Head of Perseus r., wearing winged helmet surmounted by vulture's head; in front, harpa.	CЄPЄI ΦIωN Harpa l.: border of dots [Pl. xxvii. 8.]

No.	Wt.	Metal. Size.	Obverse.	Reverse.
			SIPHNOS.	
			Seventh and Sixth centuries B.C.	
			SILVER.	
1	196·6	AR ·75	Eagle flying r.	Incuse square, quartered and divided diagonally. [Pl. XXVII. 9.]
2	171·7	AR ·8	Similar.	Similar.
3	44·6	AR ·45	Similar.	Similar. [Pl. XXVII. 10]
			Fifth century B.C., *early* (?).	
			SILVER.	
4	186·4	AR 1·	Female head r.; hair short and bound with cord (Artemis ?).	Φ Ι Σ Eagle flying r.; above head, barleycorn: the whole in incuse square. [Pl. XXVII 11.]
5	61·4	AR ·65	Similar.	Similar. [Pl. XXVII. 12.]
6	60·4	AR ·55	Similar.	Similar.
7	8·4	AR ·3	Similar.	[Σ Ι ?] Φ Similar. [Pl. XXVII. 13.]
			Fourth century B.C.	
			BRONZE.	
8		Æ ·6	Female head r.; hair rolled (Artemis ?).	ΣΙ Φ Eagle, head l., with serpent in beak. [Pl. XXVII. 14.]
9		Æ ·6	Similar.	Similar. [Pl. XXVII. 15.]
10		Æ ·65	Similar.	Similar.

No.	Wt.	Metal. Size.	Obverse.	Reverse.
			Imperial Times.	
11		Æ ·65	ΠΟ ϘΗ? Helmeted female bust r. (Pallas or Roma): border of dots.	CIΦΝΙΩΝ Eagle r., wings closed. [Pl. XXVII. 16.]
			Imperial Coinage.	
			Gordian III.	
12		Æ 1·15	[Α]ΥΤ ΚΜ ΑΝ[Τ] ΓΟΡΔΙΑ[ΝΟC] Bust of Gordian III. r.	CIΦΝΙ ΩΝ Pallas r., helmeted, holding shield in l., and spear (?) in upraised r.

No.	Wt.	Metal. Size.	Obverse.	Reverse.

SYROS.

Third, Second and First centuries B.C.

BRONZE.

No.	Wt.	Metal. Size.	Obverse.	Reverse.
1		Æ ·7	Bearded head r., horned, bound with taenia.	ΣYPI Goat l.; in front, ear of bearded wheat, erect. [Pl. XXVII. 17.]
2		Æ ·6	Similar.	ΣYPIΩN Similar.
3		Æ ·7	Similar.	Similar. [Pl. XXVII. 18.]
4		Æ ·5	Bearded head r., horned, bound with taenia.	ΣYPI Goat l. [Pl. XXVII. 19.]
5		Æ ·5	Similar.	Inscription not legible. Similar; in ex., ear of bearded wheat. [Pl. XXVII. 20.]
6		Æ ·5	Similar.	ΣYPIΩN Similar; in front, grain of corn and uncertain monogram; another monogram or letter between goat's legs. [Pl. XXVII. 21.]
7		Æ ·45	Similar.	ΣYPI Goat r.
8		Æ ·4	Similar.	ΣYP I Similar; in front, ear of wheat.
9		Æ ·4	Similar.	ΣYPI Goat r. [Pl. XXVII. 22.]

No.	Wt.	Metal. Size.	Obverse.	Reverse.
10		Æ ·7	Bearded head r., horned, bound with taenia.	ΣΥ ΡΙ Goat r.; in front, ear of bearded wheat. (Countermark, bee). [Pl. XXVIII. 1.]
11		Æ ·65	Similar.	ΣΥΡΙ Similar (same countermark).
12		Æ ·65	Similar.	Similar (same countermark). [Pl. XXVIII. 2.]
13		Æ ·45	Head of one of the Cabiri r., wearing pileus adorned with wreath.	ΣΥ Goat recumbent l. [Pl. XXVIII. 3.]
14		Æ ·4	Pilei surmounted by stars.	ΣΥΡΙ Panther running r.; between his legs, ΜΚ (?). [Pl. XXVIII. 4.]
15		Æ ·45	Similar.	Similar.
16		Æ ·5	Bee.	Σ Υ Pileus surmounted by star. [Pl. XXVIII. 5.]
17		Æ ·45	Similar.	Similar.
18		Æ ·45	Female head r., with hair tied in bunch behind (Artemis ?).	ΣΥ within wreath.
19		Æ ·65	Head of Demeter or Persephone r., wreathed with corn.	Σ Υ Ρ Two male figures (the Cabiri) standing facing, their right hands resting on their hips; the figure on the l. places l. hand on spear (?), the figure on the r. has his l. hand outstretched. [Pl. XXVIII. 6.]
20		Æ ·55	Head of Hermes r., wearing petasos.	Σ Υ Ρ Ι Caduceus.

No.	Wt.	Metal. Size.	Obverse.	Reverse.
			Imperial Coinage.	
			Domitian.	
21		Æ ·85	ΚΑΙCΑΡ ΑΥΓΟΥC-ΤΟC ΔΟΜΙΤΙΑ ΝΟC Head of Domitian r., laur.	CΥ [ΡΙ] ΚΑ Β[Ι]Ρ Two heads facing one another (Domitian and Domitia ?); between them, ear of bearded wheat; beneath, star and bee. [Pl. XXVIII. 7.]
22		Æ ·85	Similar.	CΥ [ΡΙ] ΚΑΒ ΙΡΩ Ν Similar; beneath, bee and star.
			Trajan.	
23		Æ ·7	·ΥΚ Μ· ΤRΑΙΑΝΟC ? Head of Trajan r., laur.	ЄΙCΙC ИΩΙϤV[Ɔ] Head of Isis r.; hair in long curls; lotus-flower on head.
			Antoninus Pius.	
24		Æ ·85	ΑVΤ·ΚΑΙ·CЄΒ·ΑΝ-ΤωΝЄΙΝ ΟC Head of Antoninus Pius r., laur.	CV ΡΙ ΚΑΒ ΙΡΩ Ν Two heads facing one another (Faustina jun. and M. Aurelius ?); between them, ear of bearded wheat; beneath, bee and star. [Pl. XXVIII. 8.]
			M. Aurelius and L. Verus.	
25		Æ ·85	(ΑΥ ?) .ΥΗΡΟCΑ.. ΑΝΤ[ΩΝЄΙ]ΝΟ[C] Heads of M. Aurelius and L. Verus, facing one another.	Κ Α ΒΙ CΥΡΙωИ Two heads facing one another (Commodus and Crispina ?); between them, date-palm.
26		Æ ·85	ΑΥ.... ΗΡΟC Α[ΝΤ] ΩΝЄΙΝΟC Heads of M. Aurelius and L. Verus, facing one another.	CΥΡ [Ι] ωИ Head of Isis r.; hair in long curls; lotus-flower on head.

No.	Wt.	Metal. Size.	Obverse.	Reverse.
			L. Verus.	
27		Æ ·8	ΟΥΗΡΟϹ ΚΑΙϹΑΡ Head of L. Verus r., beardless.	ϹΥ ΡΙ ΚΑΒ ΙΡΩ Ν Two heads facing another (Fau jun. and M. A lius?); between them, ear bearded wheat; beneath, bee star.
			Commodus.	
28		Æ ·75	VAA ƆOΔOMOꓘ Head of Commodus r., laur.	ИωΙ ꟼVƆ Isis l., holding i sistrum. [Pl. XXVIII. 9.]
			Sept. Severus.	
29		Æ ·75	ΑΥ·ΚΑΙ·ϹЄ(ϹЄΟΥ-ΗΡΟϹ?) Head of Sept. Severus r.	ЄΡΜΗϹ ϹΥΡΙΩΝ Herme holding purse and caduceus.

No.	Wt.	Metal. Size.	Obverse.	Reverse.

TENOS.

Fourth century B.C.

SILVER.

No.	Wt.	Metal. Size.	Obverse.	Reverse.
1	253·6	AR 1·	Head of bearded Zeus Ammon r., laur.	T H Poseidon, wearing himation over lower limbs, seated l., holding in outstretched r., dolphin; his l. resting on trident. [Pl. XXVIII. 10.]
2	63·8	AR ·6	Similar.	T H Bunch of grapes with two leaves. [Pl. XXVIII. 11.]

BRONZE.

No.	Wt.	Metal. Size.	Obverse.	Reverse.
3		Æ ·4	Head of bearded Zeus Ammon r., laur.: plain border.	T H Bunch of grapes with two leaves. [Pl. XXVIII. 12.]
4		Æ ·45	Similar type.	Similar. [Pl. XXVIII. 13.]
5		Æ ·6	Head of bearded Zeus Ammon r., laur.	T H Trident upwards. [Pl. XXVIII. 14.]
6		Æ ·75	Head of bearded Zeus Ammon r., laur.	T H Bunch of grapes. [Pl. XXVIII. 15.]

No.	Wt.	Metal. Size.	Obverse.	Reverse.
			Third and Second centuries B.C.	
			SILVER	
7	106·1	AR ·8	Head of young Zeus Ammon r., laur.	ΤΗΝΙΩΝ Poseidon standin wearing himation which le the right arm and the upper of his body bare, holding in stretched r., dolphin; his l. on trident; in field l., buncl grapes. [Pl. XXVIII. 17.]
8	35·2	AR ·6	Similar.	T H N I Bunch of grapes. [Pl. XXVIII. 16.]
			BRONZE.	
9		Æ ·7	Head of young Zeus Ammon r., laur. (Countermark, dolphin r.).	[N I] T [H] Bunch of grapes, to which, trident.
10		Æ ·65	Similar (no countermark).	N I T H Similar. [Pl. XXVIII. 18.]
11		Æ ·65	Similar.	Similar. [Pl. XXVIII. 19.]
12		Æ ·65	Similar.	Similar.
13		Æ ·65	Similar.	[T H] N I Similar. [Pl. XXVIII. 20.]

No.	Wt.	Metal. Size.	Obverse.	Reverse.
4		Æ ·6	Head of young Zeus Ammon r., laur.	T H Trident upwards, on each side of which, dolphin, upwards.
5		Æ ·6	Similar.	Similar. [Pl. xxix. 1.]
6		Æ ·65	Head of bearded Zeus Ammon r, laur.	T H Thyrsus within wreath of ivy-leaves and berries. [Pl. xxix. 2.]
17		Æ ·6	Head of bearded Zeus Ammon r., laur.	T H Bunch of grapes.
18		Æ ·5	Similar.	Similar.
19		Æ ·5	Similar.	T H N I Similar. [Pl. xxix. 3.]
20		Æ ·75	Head of Poseidon r., laur.	T H N [I] Trident; on each side of its handle, dolphin, upwards; in field l., rose. [Pl. xxix. 4.]
21		Æ ·75	Similar. (Countermark, dolphin r.).	T H N I Similar.
22		Æ ·75	Similar (no countermark).	Similar; no symbol visible.
23		Æ ·65	Similar.	T H N I Trident; on each side of its handle, dolphin, downwards; in field r., rose.
24		Æ ·65	Similar.	Similar. [Pl. xxix. 5.]
25		Æ ·65	Similar.	T H N I Trident; on each side of its handle, dolphin, upwards. [Pl. xxix. 6.]

No.	Wt.	Metal. Size.	Obverse.	Reverse.
26		Æ ·65	Head of Apollo r., laur.	N I [T] H Bunch of grapes. [Pl. xxix. 7.]
27		Æ ·7	Head of young Zeus Ammon r., laur.	THNIΩN Poseidon stand wearing himation, holding t in r.; his l. on hip; in field l. [Pl. xxix. 8.]
28		Æ ·85	Similar. (Countermark, bunch of grapes).	Similar.
29		Æ ·75	Similar (same countermark).	ИΩI[ИHT] Poseidon r., w himation, holding in r., tr his l. on hip; at his foot, dolp
30		Æ ·75	Similar (no countermark).	[И]ΩIИHT Similar.
31		Æ ·7	Similar.	THNIΩN Poseidon stand wearing himation, holding i stretched r., dolphin, in l., tr in field l., rose. [Pl. xxix. 9.]
32		Æ ·65	Similar. (Countermark, bunch of grapes).	Similar.
33		Æ ·85	THNIΩ[N] Poseidon l., wearing himation, holding in r., trident, to the lower part of which clings a dolphin; his l. on hip.	Dionysos r., wearing himation ing back; his r. is upraised holds thyrsus; in field l., in field r., dolphin, downwa [Pl. xxix. 10.]
34		Æ ·8	Similar.	Similar.

Wt.	Metal. Size.	Obverse.	Reverse.
	Æ ·55	Head of young Zeus Ammon r., laur.	T H N I Trident; on each side of its handle, dolphin, downwards.
	Æ ·5	Head of bearded Zeus Ammon r., laur.	T H N I Dolphin l.
	Æ ·4	Similar.	Similar; dolphin r. [Pl. XXIX. 11.]
	Æ ·35	Similar.	Similar.
	Æ ·4	Head of Poseidon r.; behind shoulder, trident.	T H N I Dolphin r.
	Æ ·4	Similar.	Similar.
	Æ ·45	Head of Poseidon r., laur.: border of dots.	T H N I Trident; on each side of its handle, dolphin, upwards. [Pl. XXIX. 12.]
	Æ ·3	T H Bunch of grapes.	Bunch of grapes.
	Æ ·35	Similar.	Similar.

Imperial Coinage.

Sabina.

Wt.	Metal. Size.	Obverse.	Reverse.
	Æ ·7	CABЄINA [CЄBAC] TH Bust of Sabina r.	TH NI ΩN Dionysos l., wearing himation, holding in r., kantharos, in l., thyrsus.

No.	Wt.	Metal. Size.	Obverse.	Reverse.

THERA.

Third and Second centuries B.C.

BRONZE.

No.	Wt.	Metal. Size.	Obverse.	Reverse.
1		Æ ·7	Head of Apollo, three-quarter face towards l.	ΘΗ Bull butting r. [in ex., dolphins?]. [Pl. xxix. 13.]
2		Æ ·55	Head of Apollo r., laur.	ΘΗ Bull butting r. [Pl. xxix. 14.]
3		Æ ·5	Head of Apollo r., laur.	Θ Η Lyre. [Pl. xxix. 15.]
4		Æ ·6	Similar? (barbarous).	Similar. [Pl. xxix. 16.]

Imperial Coinage.

M. Aurelius.

No.	Wt.	Metal. Size.	Obverse.	Reverse.
5		Æ 1·15	AVTKMA VP[AN-[TΩNI]NOC Bust of M. Aurelius r., laur.	ΘΗΡΑΙ ΩΝ Archaic simula of Apollo radiate, naked, facin holds in r., plectrum, in l. (ly [Pl. xxix. 17.]
6		Æ 1·2	[AV]TKMA VPAN-TΩNINOC Similar.	ΘΗΡЄ ΩΝ Archaic simulac [Pl. xxix. 18.]

L. Verus.

No.	Wt.	Metal. Size.	Obverse.	Reverse.
7		Æ 1·2	AVTKMAV P OVH-POC Bust of L. Verus r., laur.	ΘΗ ΡΑΙ ΩΝ Apollo Cith dus in long flowing dress, stan facing; in his r., plectrum, in l.,

INDEX I.

GEOGRAPHICAL.

N.

O.

P.

R.

S.

T.

INDEX II.

TYPES.

B.

C.

D.

Z.

INDEX III.

REMARKABLE SYMBOLS.

INDEX IV. A.

KINGS, TYRANTS, &c.

INDEX IV. B.

MAGISTRATES' NAMES ON AUTONOMOUS COINS.

INDEX IV. C.

MAGISTRATES' NAMES ON IMPERIAL COINS.

INDEX V.

ROMAN MAGISTRATES' NAMES.

(*a. In Greek.*)

(*β. In Latin.*)

INDEX VI.

ENGRAVERS' NAMES.

INDEX VII.

REMARKABLE INSCRIPTIONS.

TABLE

FOR

CONVERTING ENGLISH INCHES INTO MILLIMÈTRES

AND THE

MEASURES OF MIONNET'S SCALE.

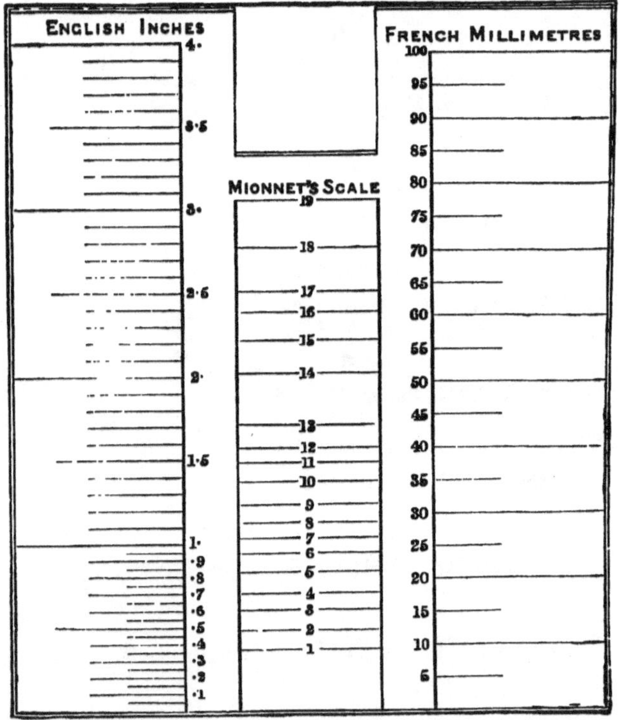

Gilbert & Rivington, Limited, 52, St. John's Square, Clerkenwell, E.C.

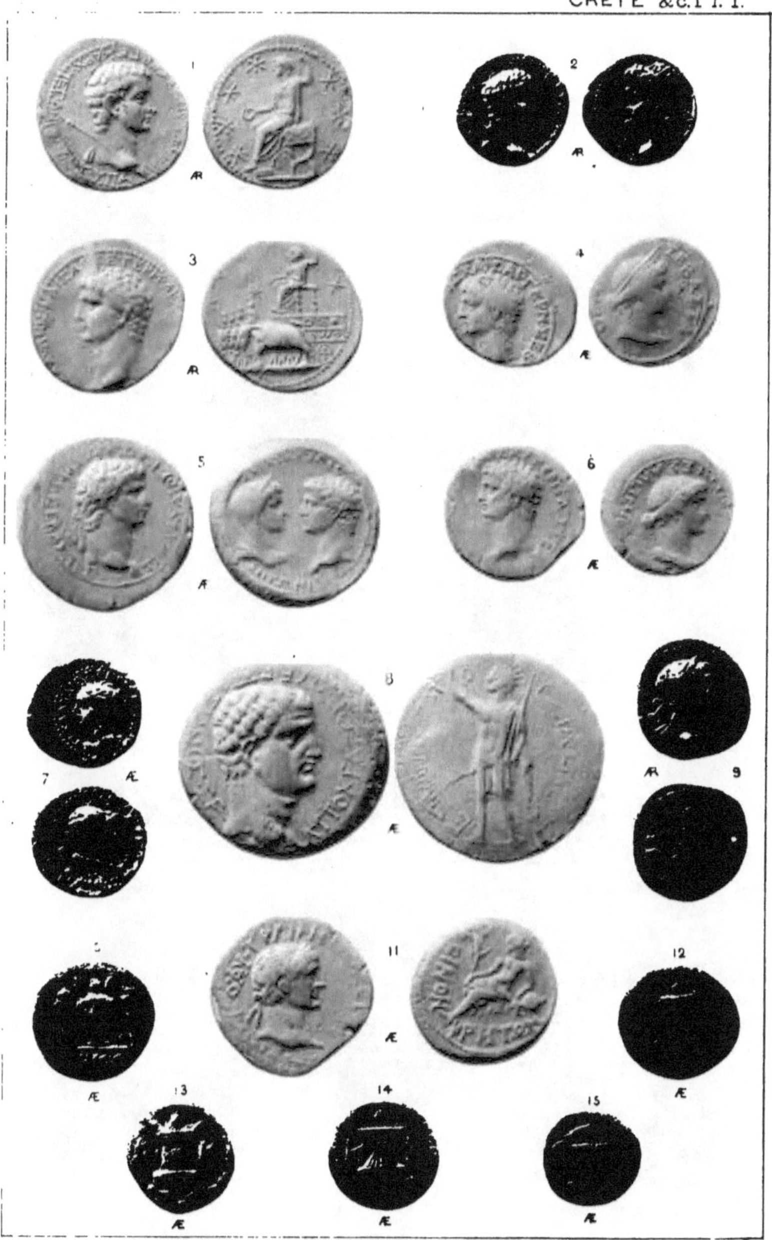

CRETE.

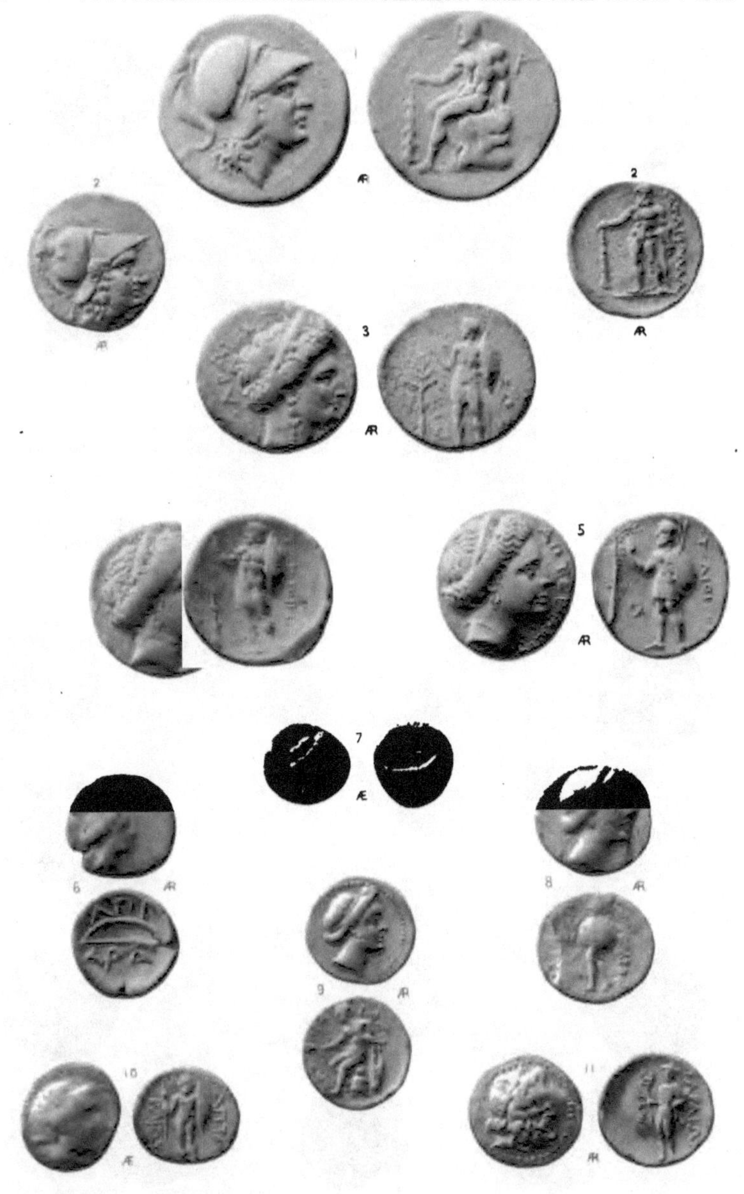

ALLARIA—APTERA.

1 Æ
2
Æ
3
Æ
4
5
Æ
Æ
6
Æ
7
AR
8
AR
9
Æ
10 Æ
11
Æ
12
AR
13
Æ
14
Æ
15
AR
16
Æ
17
Æ
18
Æ
19
Æ

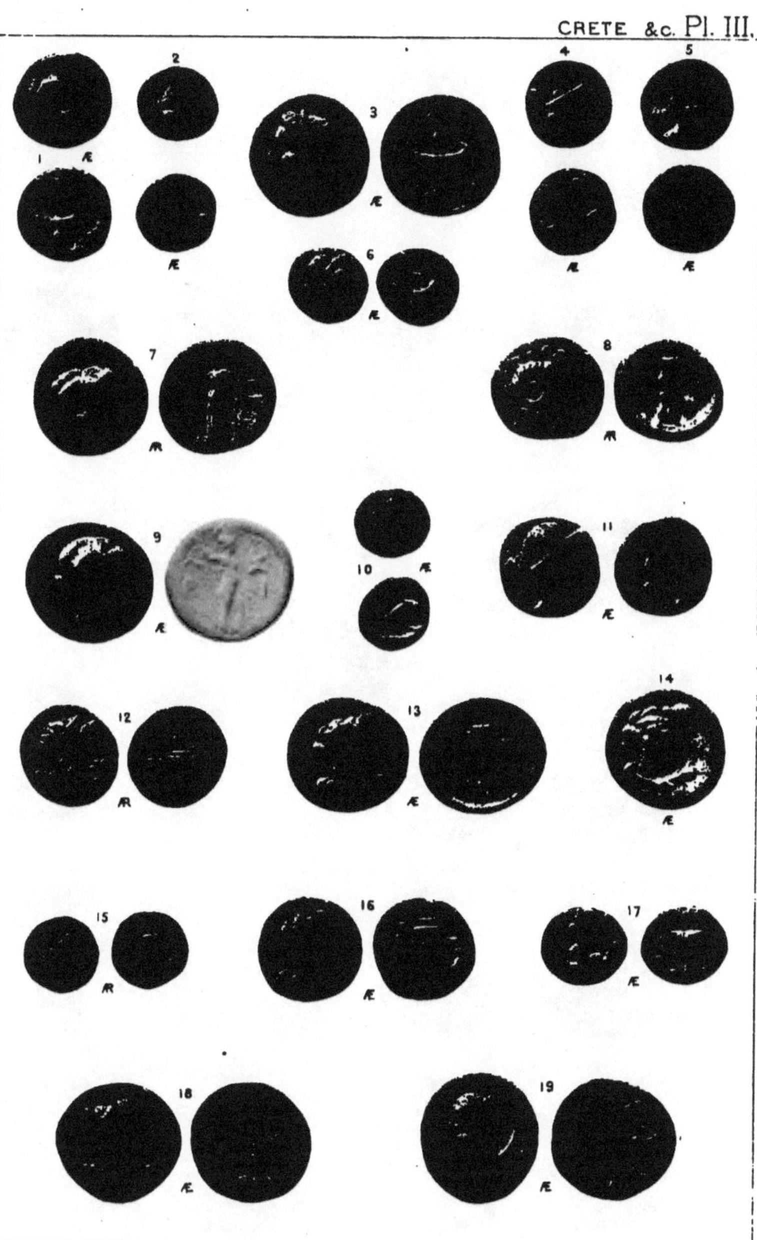

APTERA — AXUS.

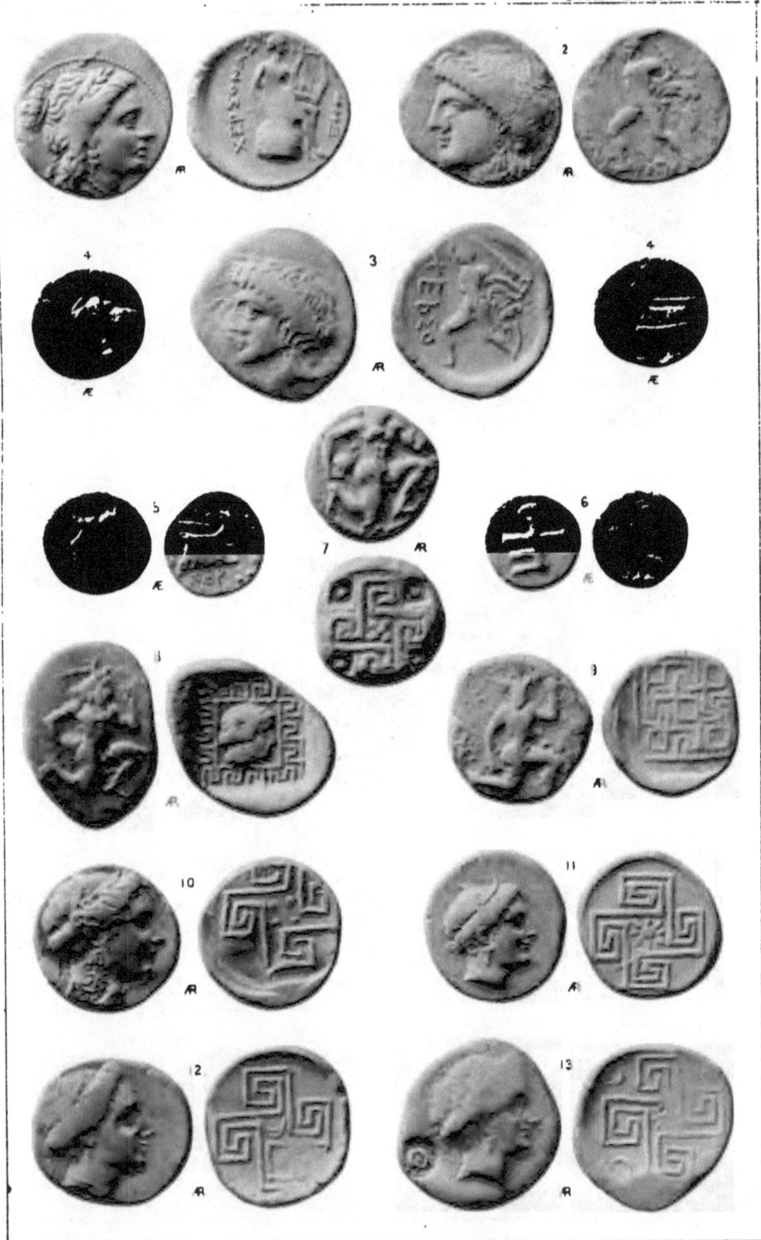

CHERSONESUS, CNOSSUS.

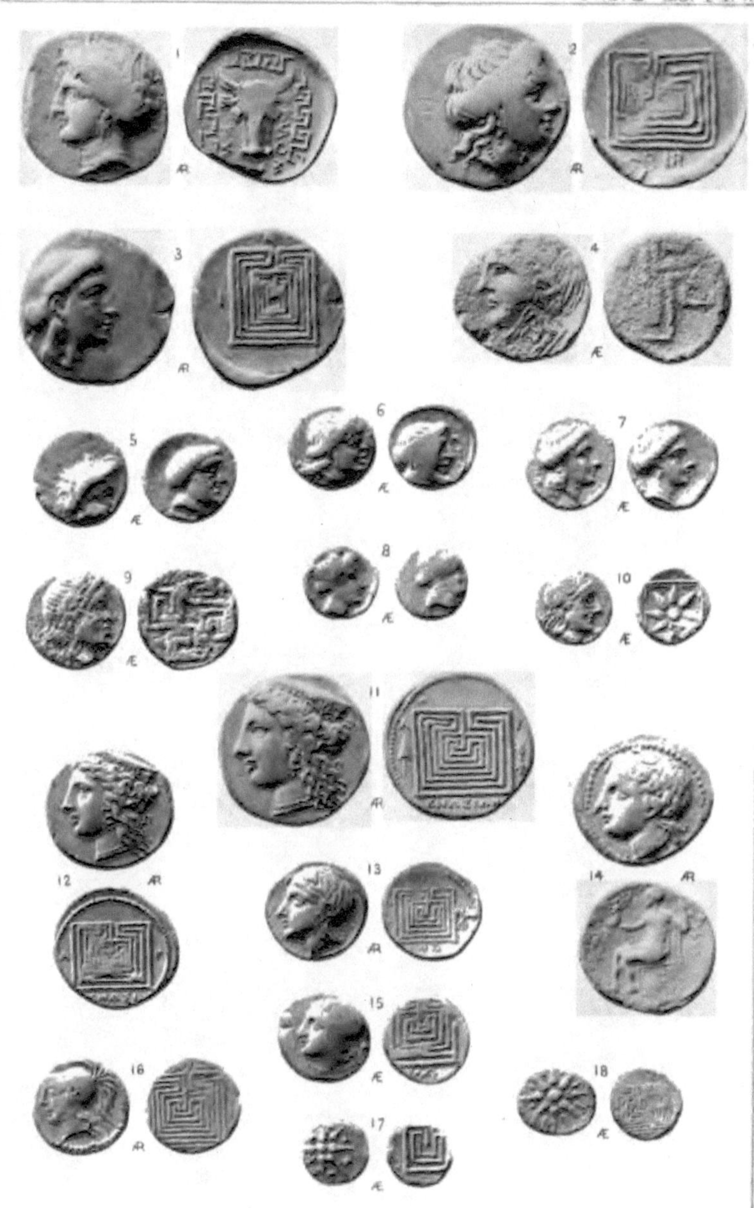

CNOSSUS.

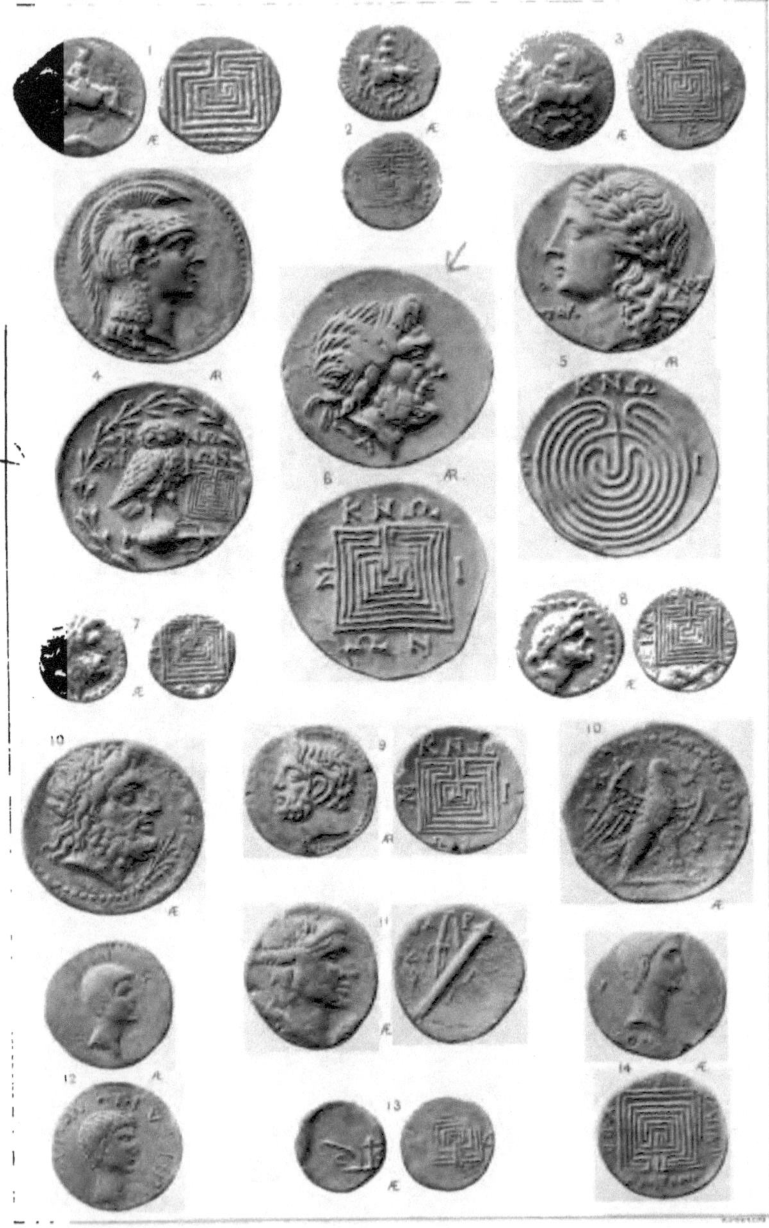

CNOSSUS.

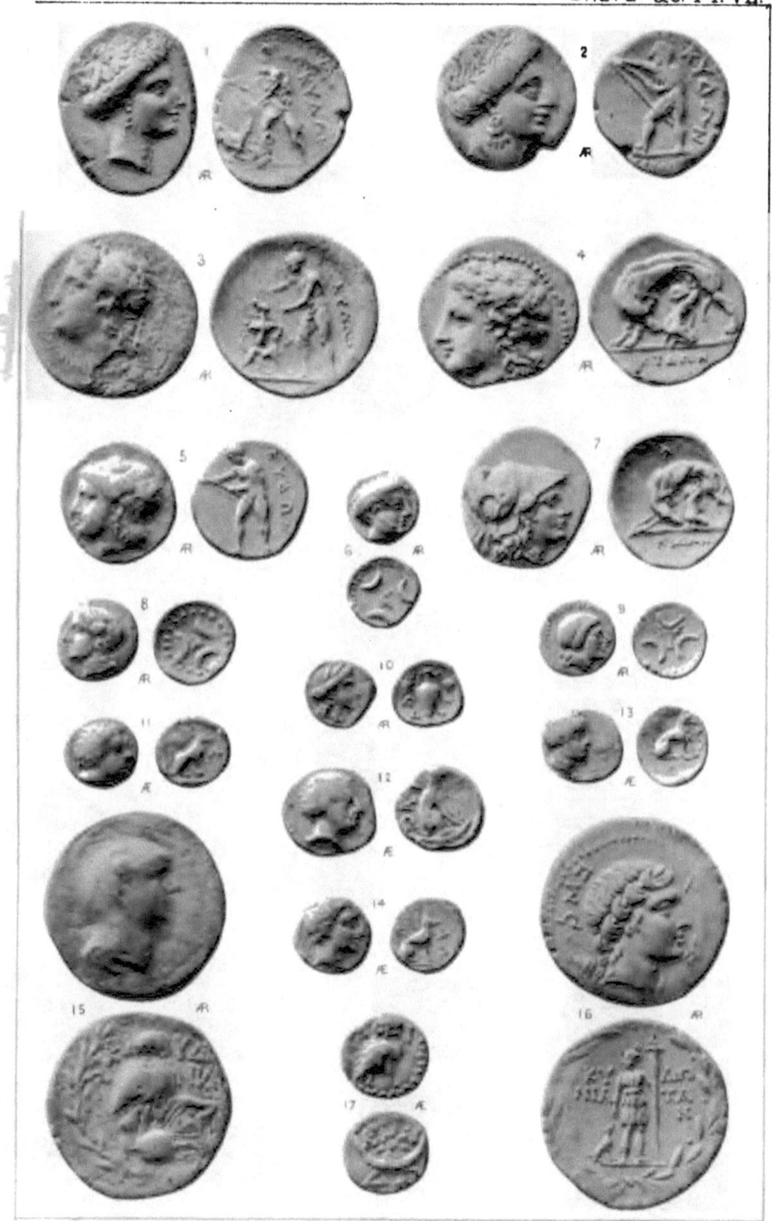

CYDONIA.

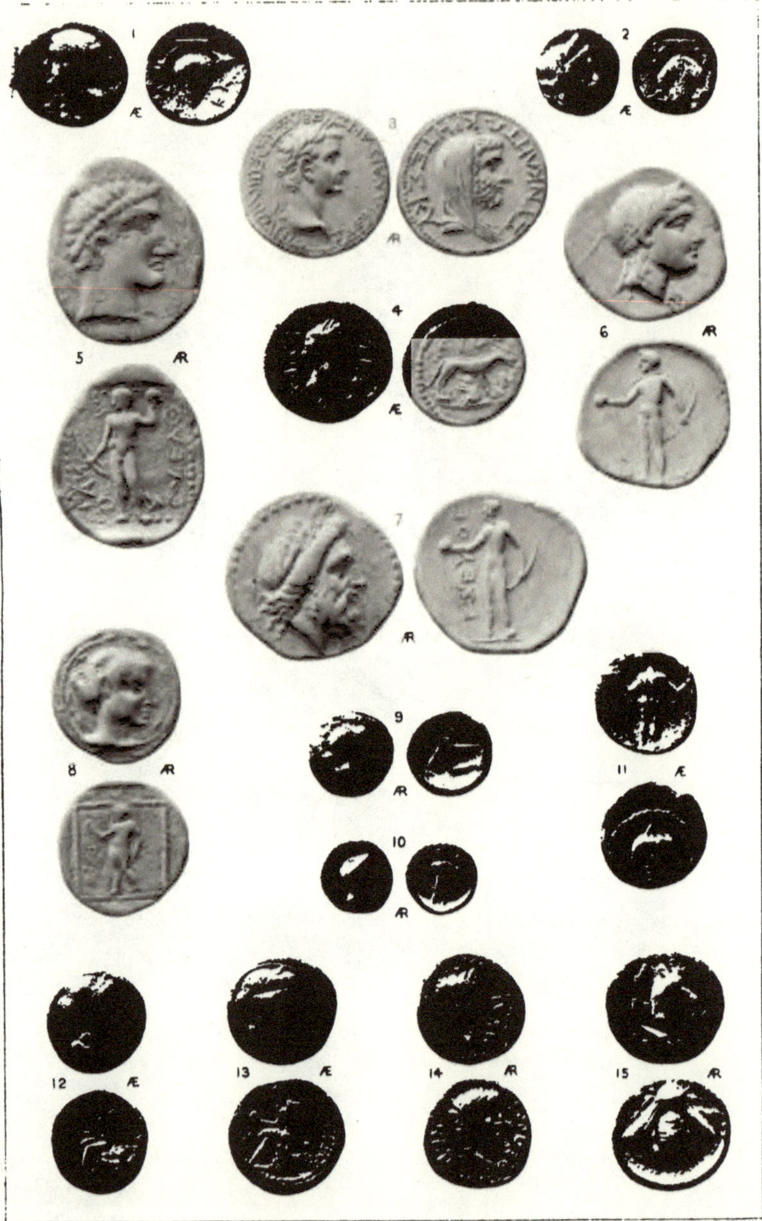

CYDONIA—ELYRUS.

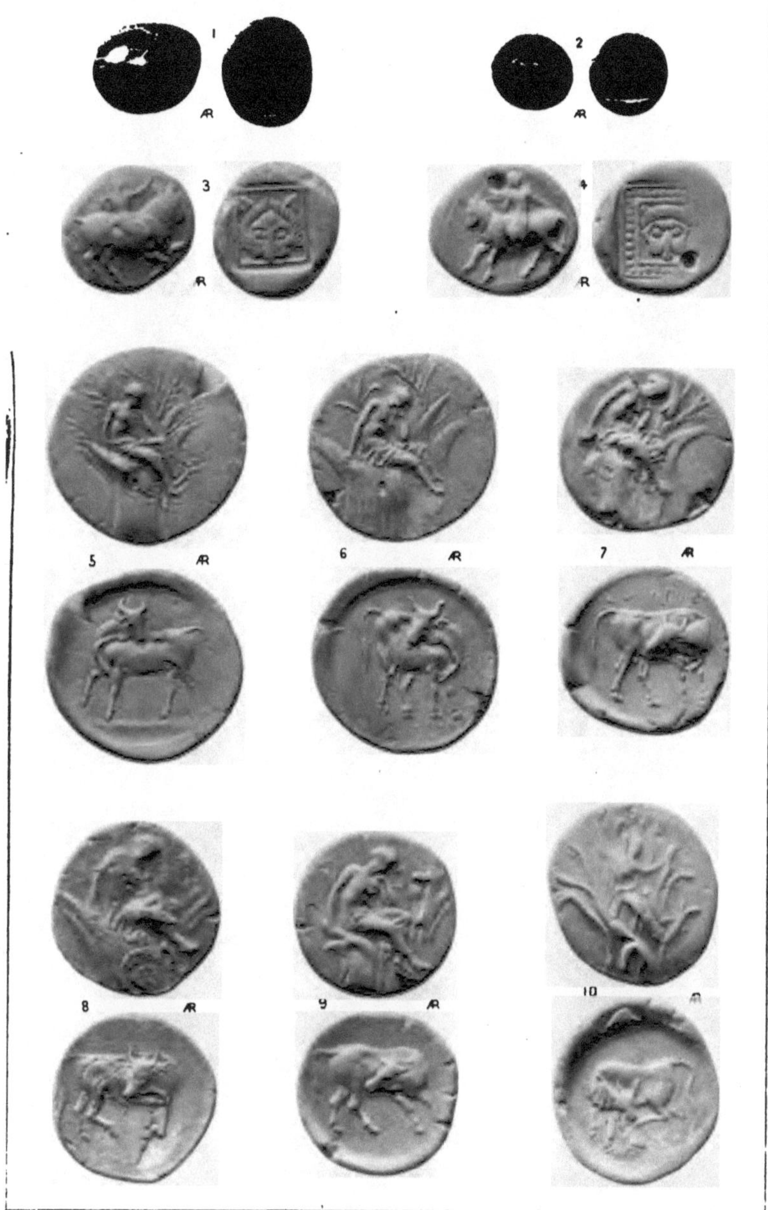

GORTYNA.

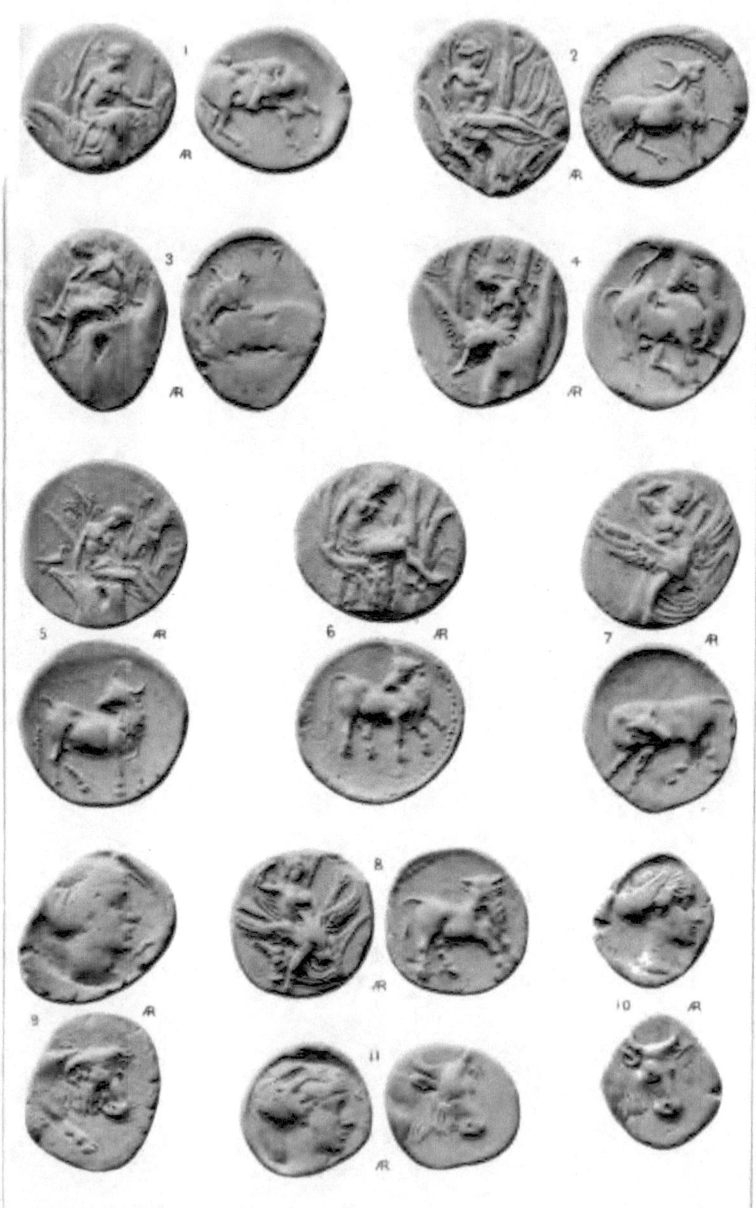

GORTYNA.

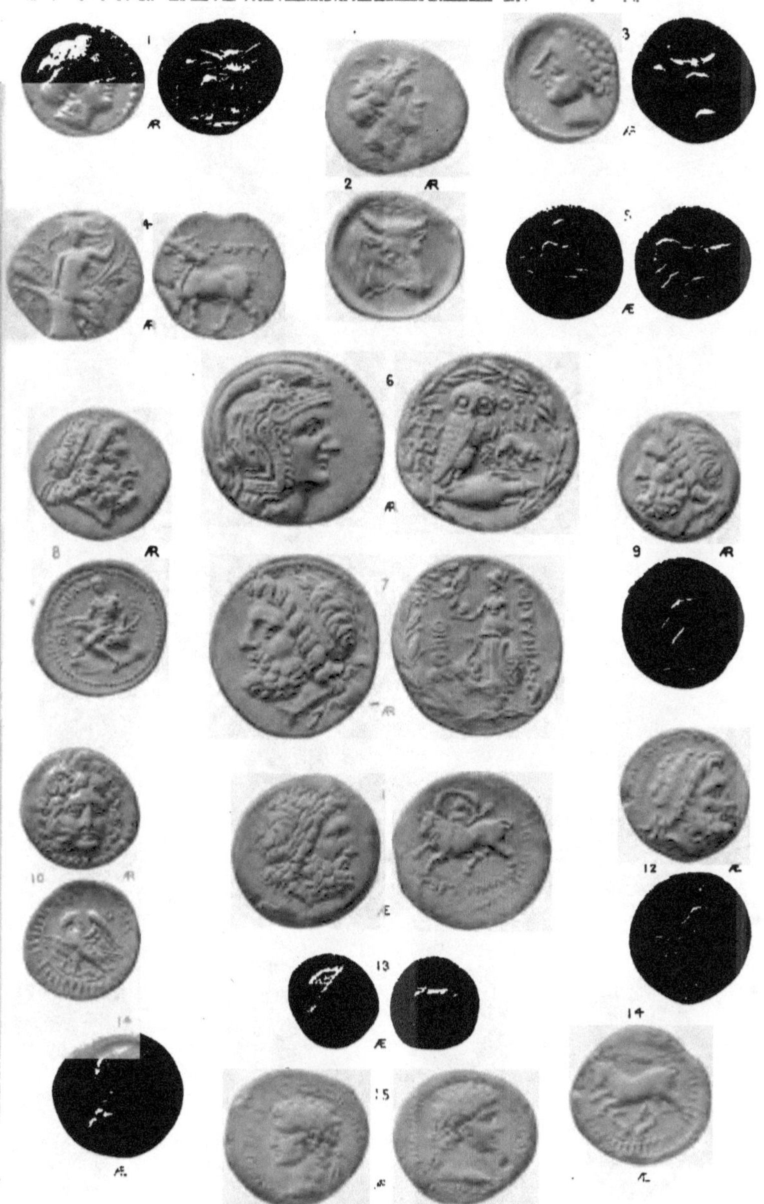

GORTYNA.

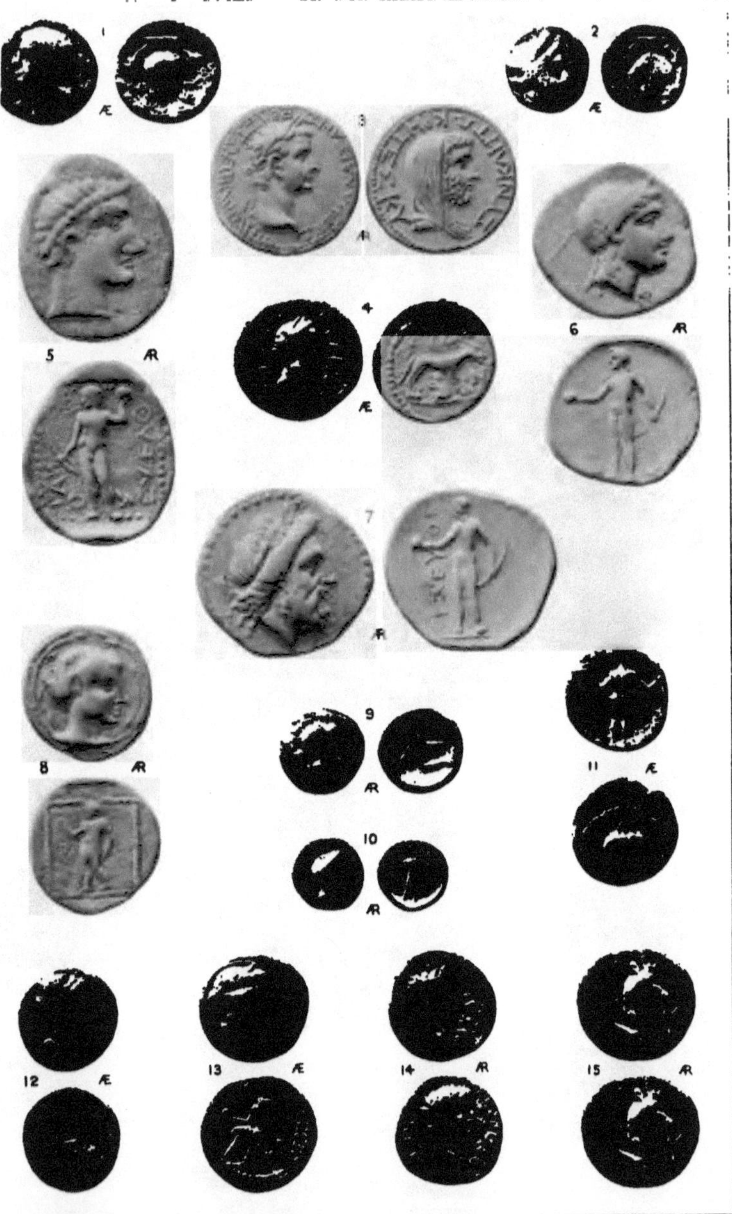

CYDONIA—ELYRUS.

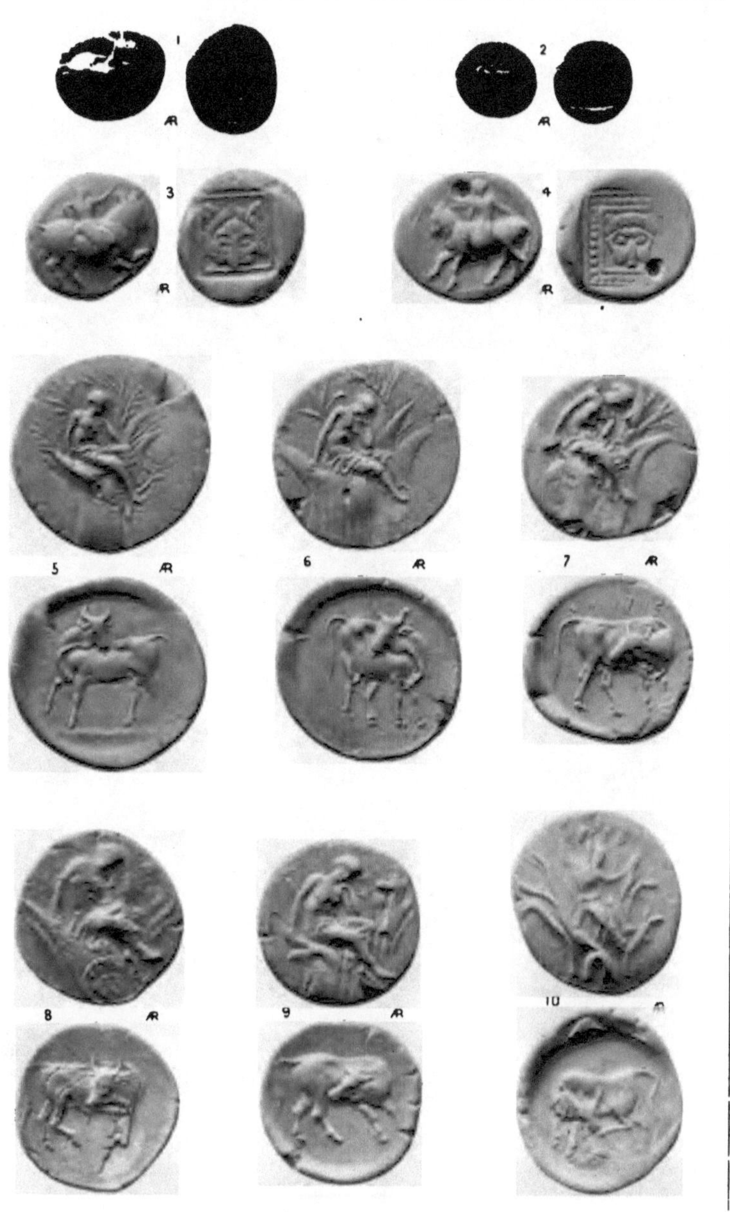

GORTYNA.

CRETE &c. Pl. X.

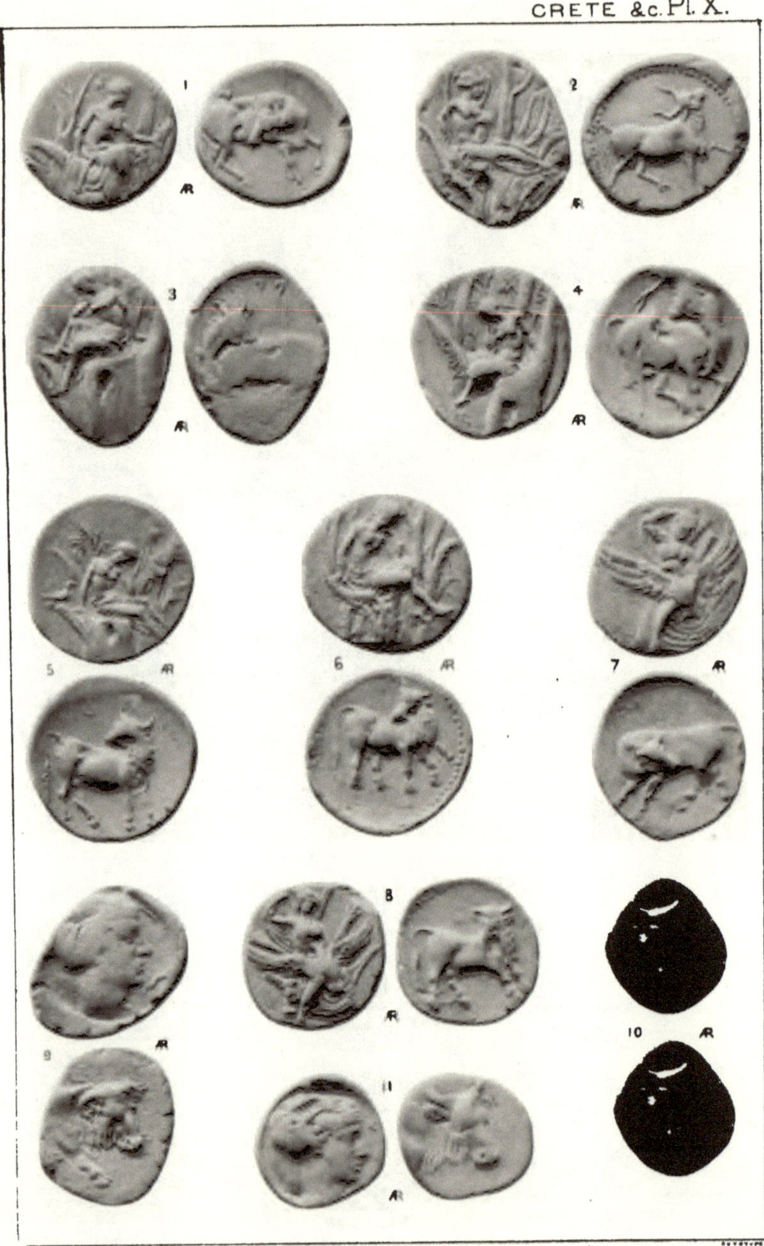

GORTYNA.

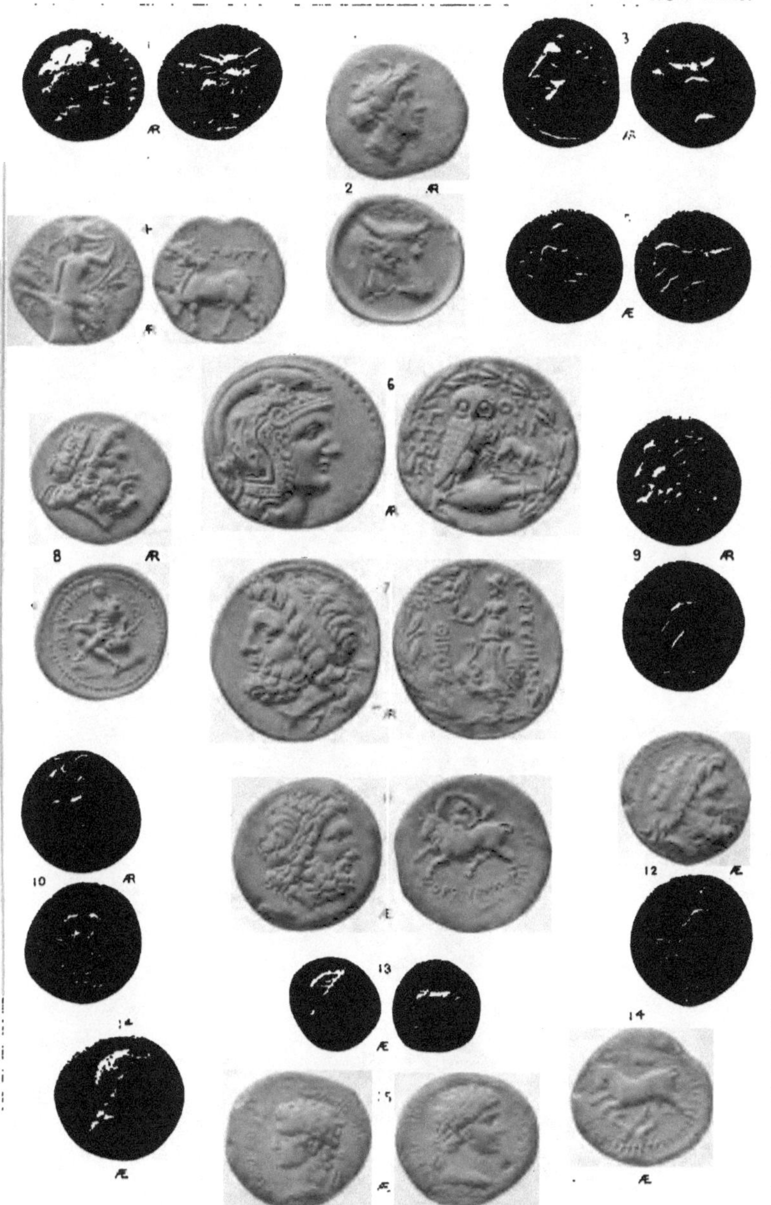

GORTYNA.

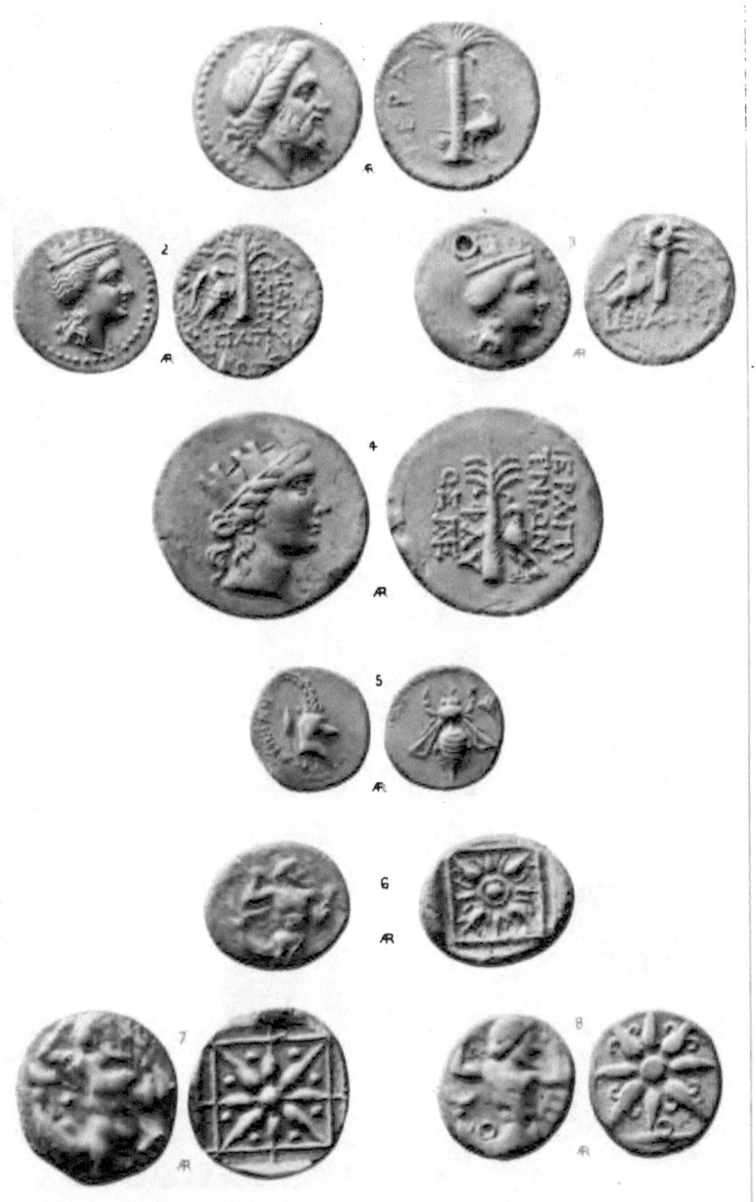

HIERAPYTNA — ITANUS.

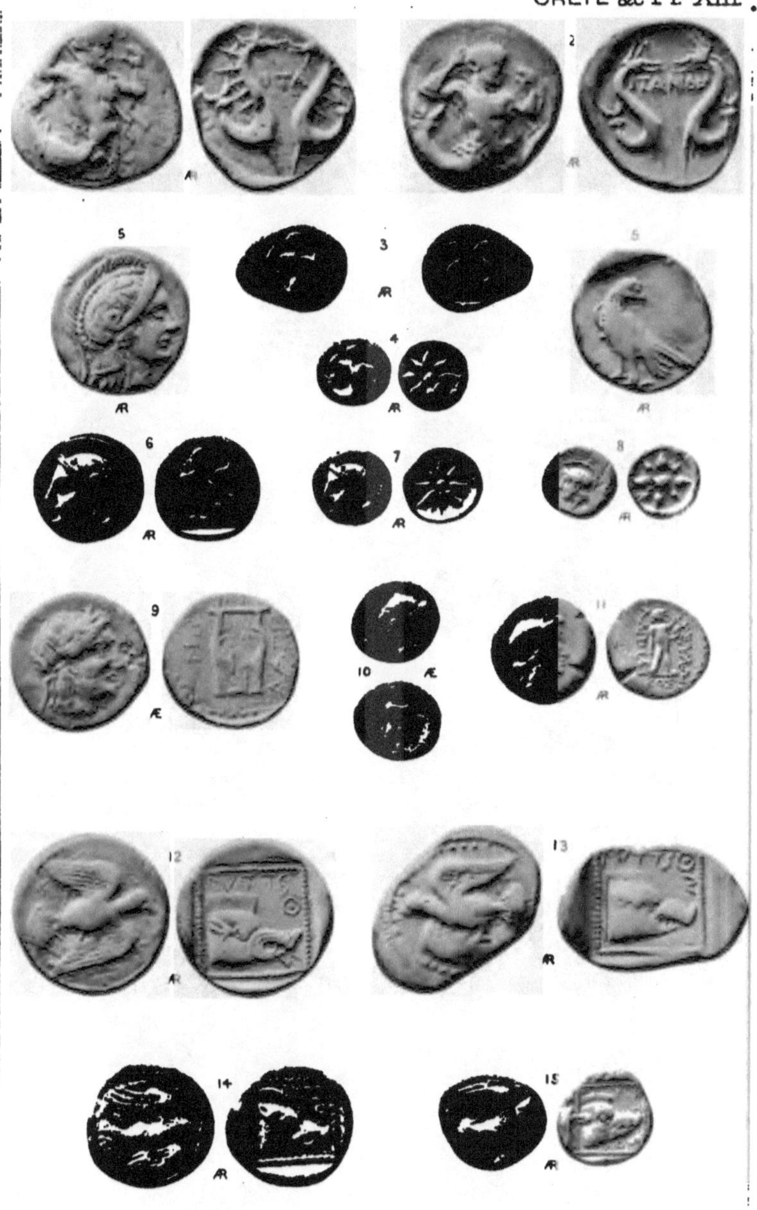

ITANUS—LYTTUS.

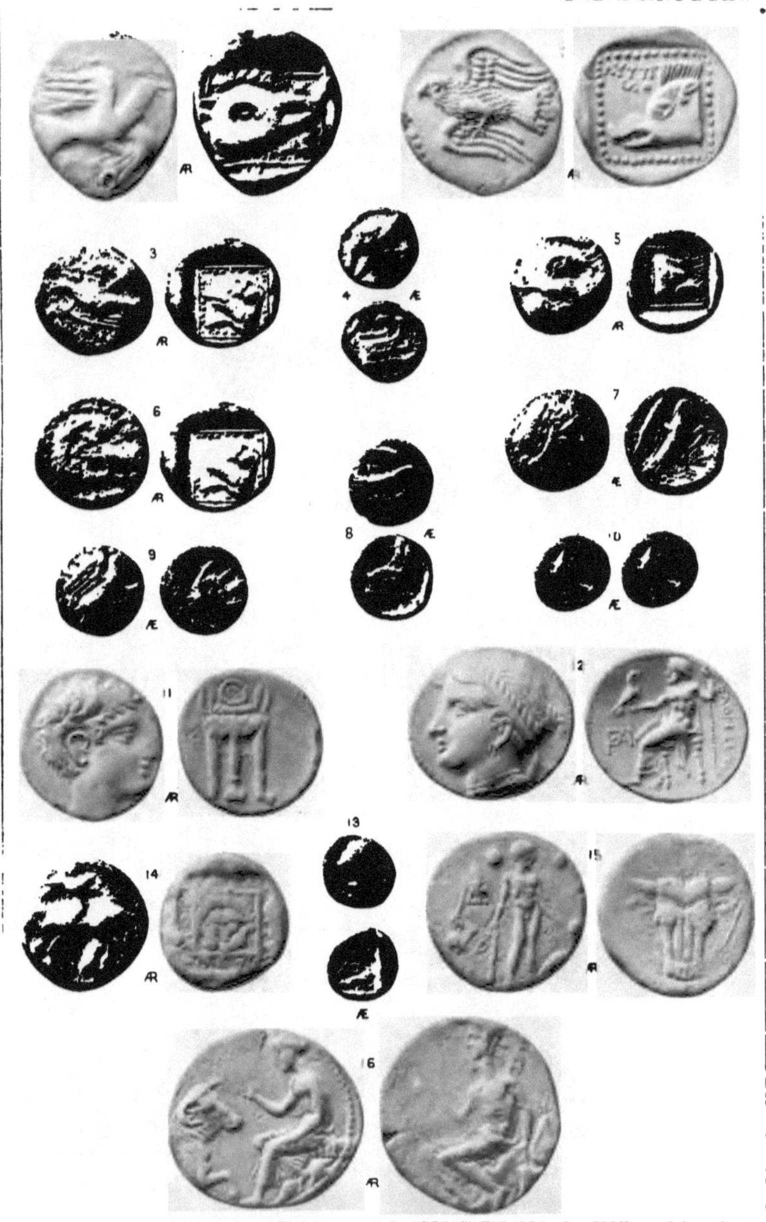

LYTTUS — PHAESTUS.

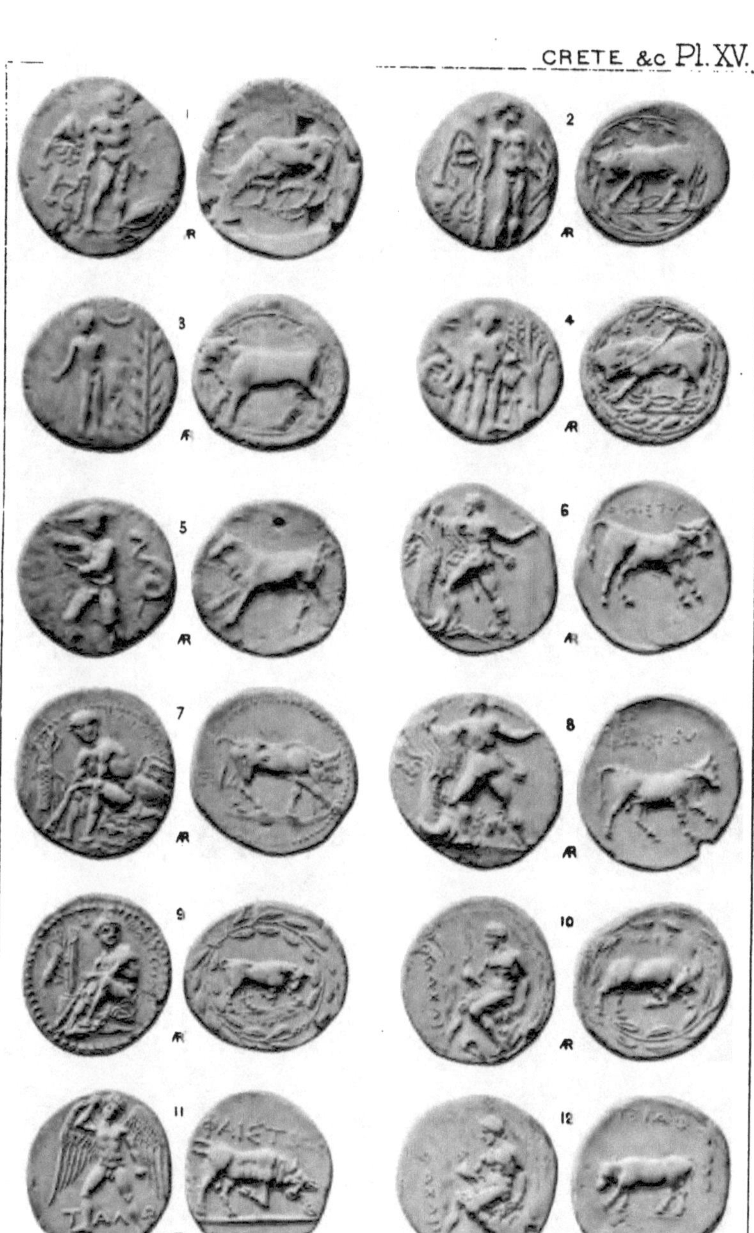

PHAESTUS.

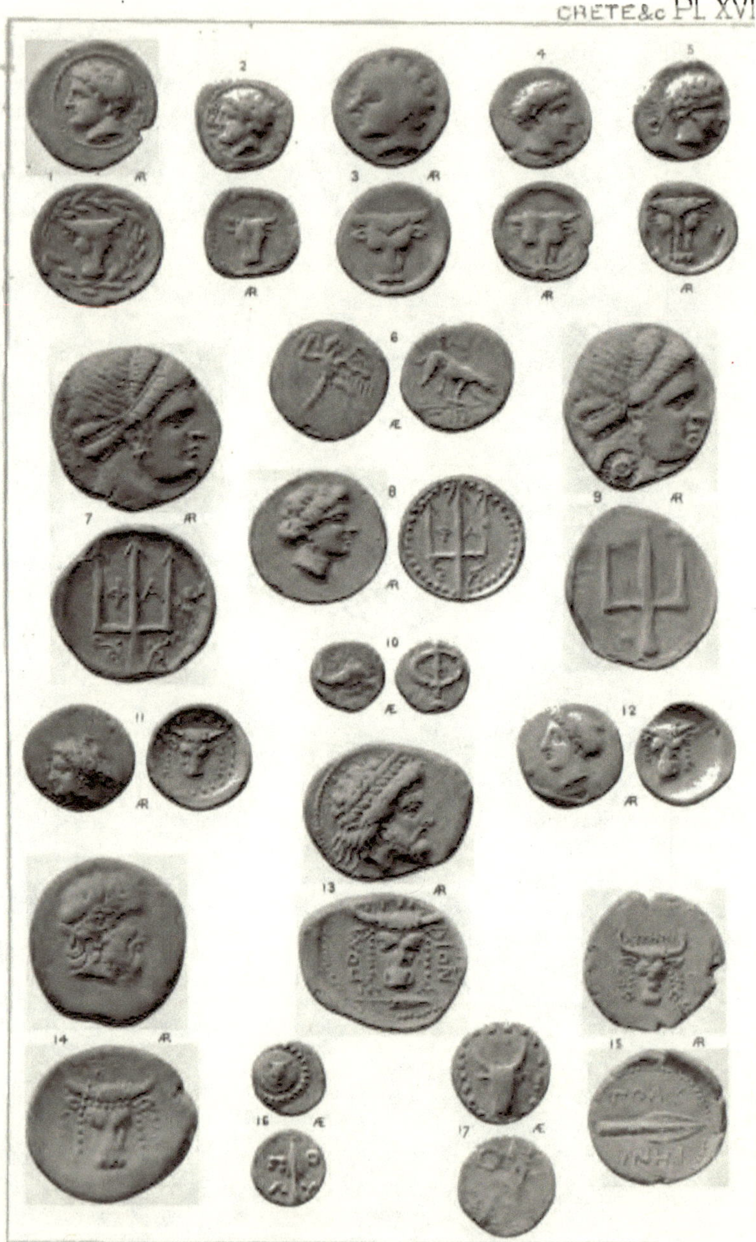

PHAESTUS — POLYRHENIUM.

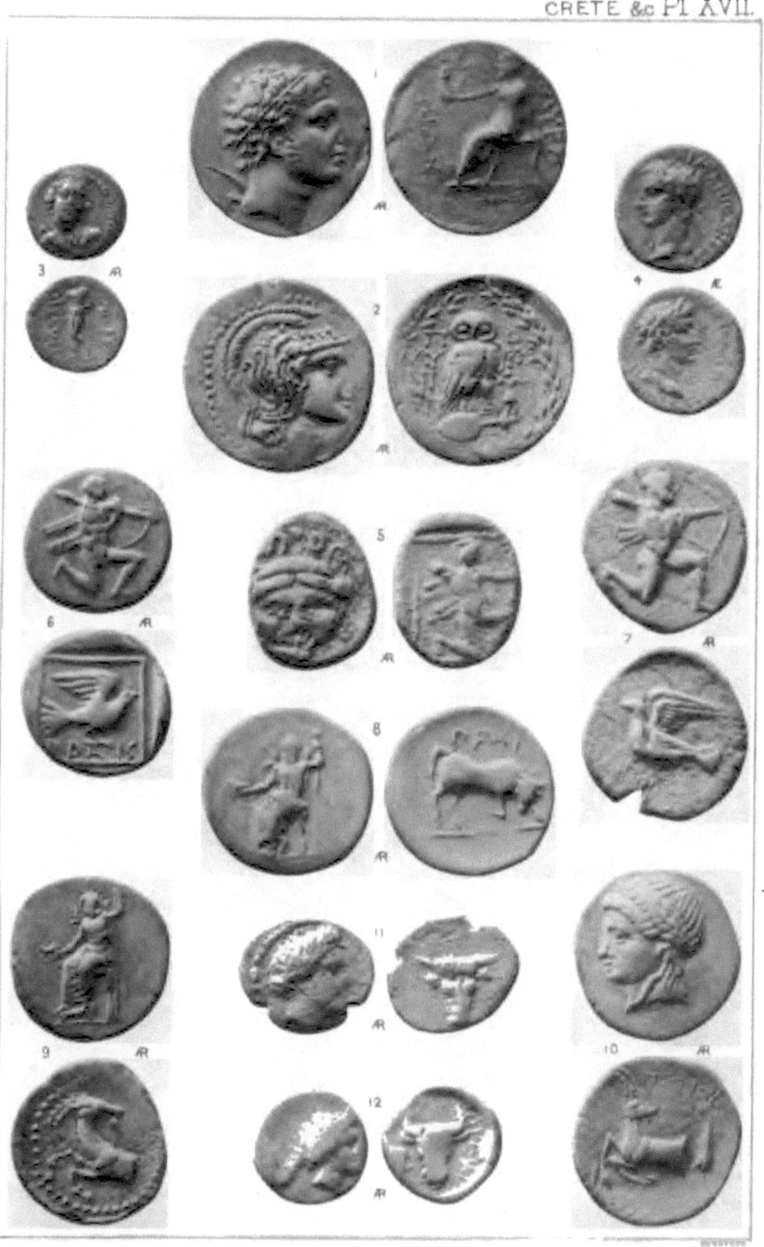

POLYRHENIUM, PRAESUS,

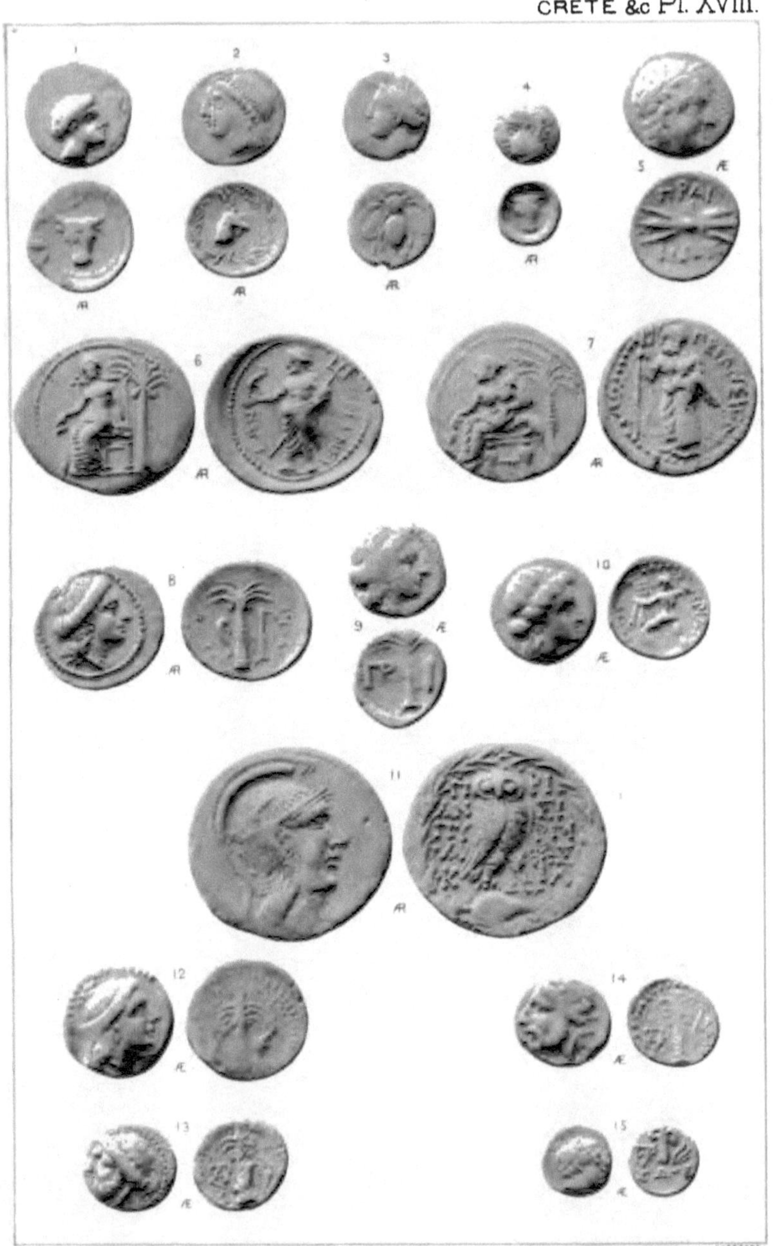

PRAESUS — PYRANTHUS.

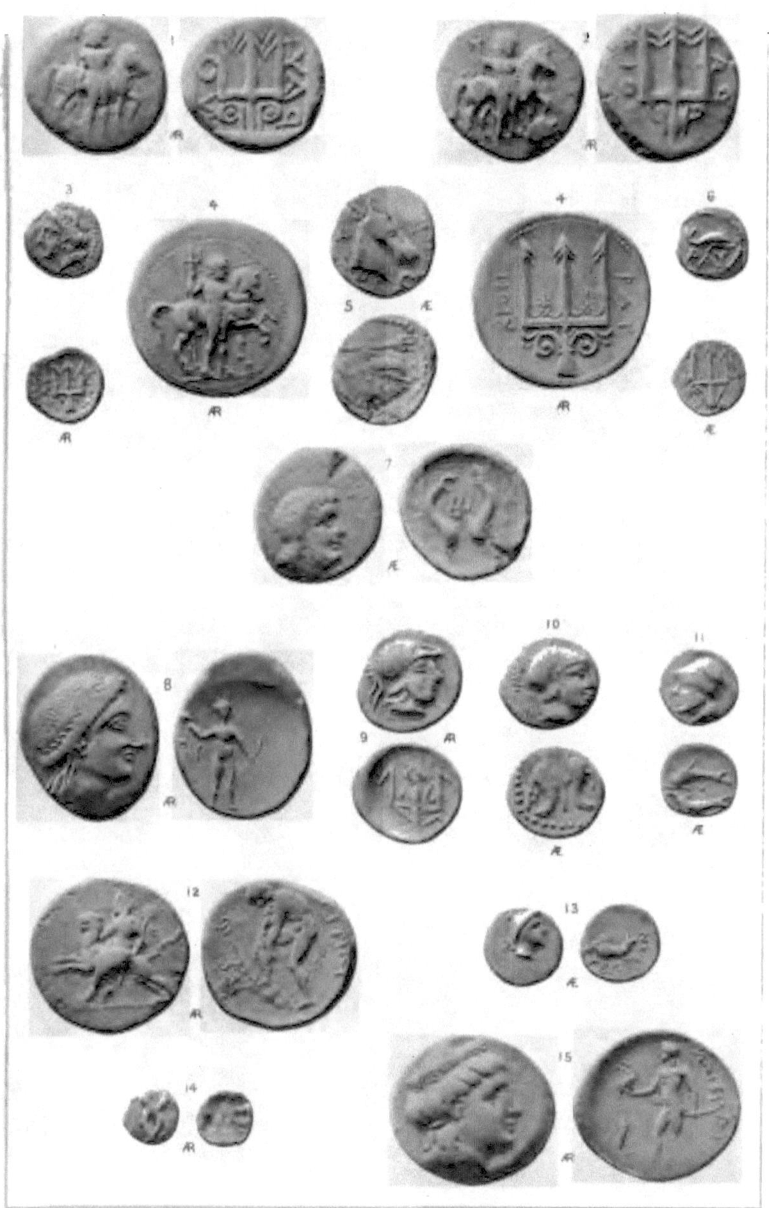

RHAUCUS — TYLISSUS.

CRETE &c Pl. XXI.

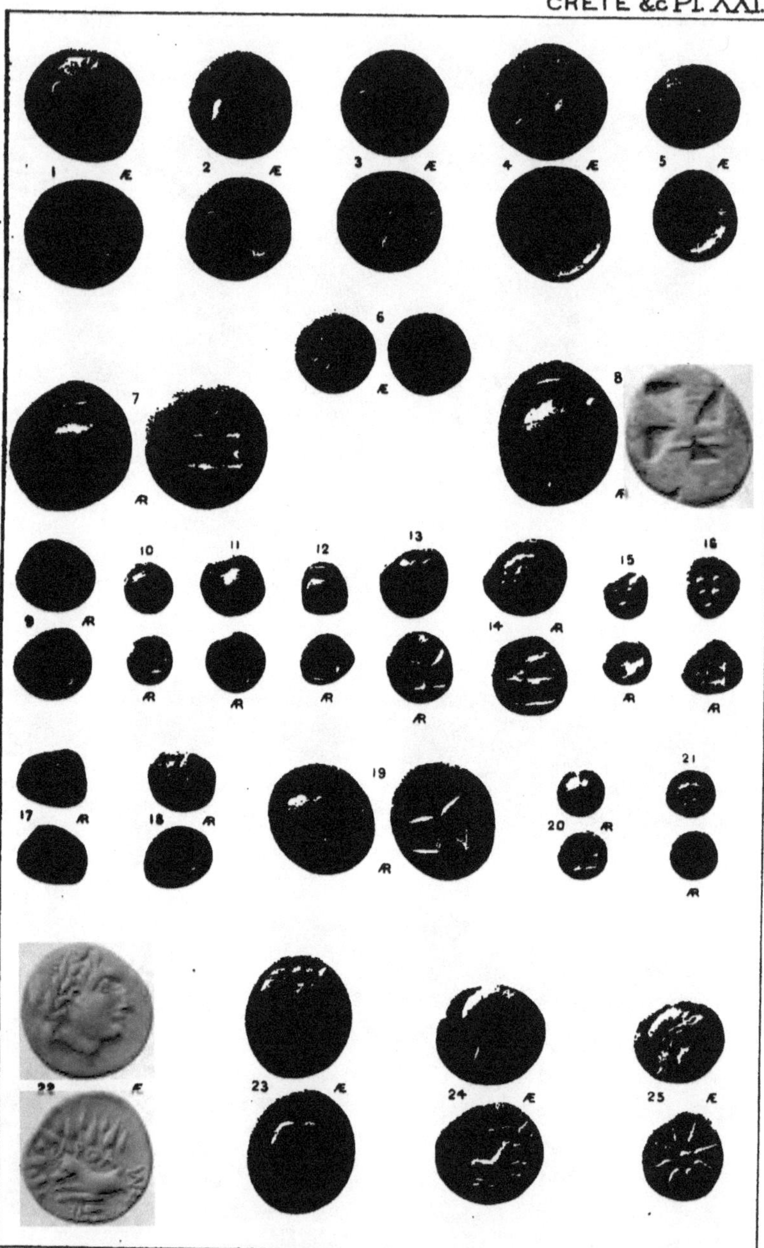

CEOS.

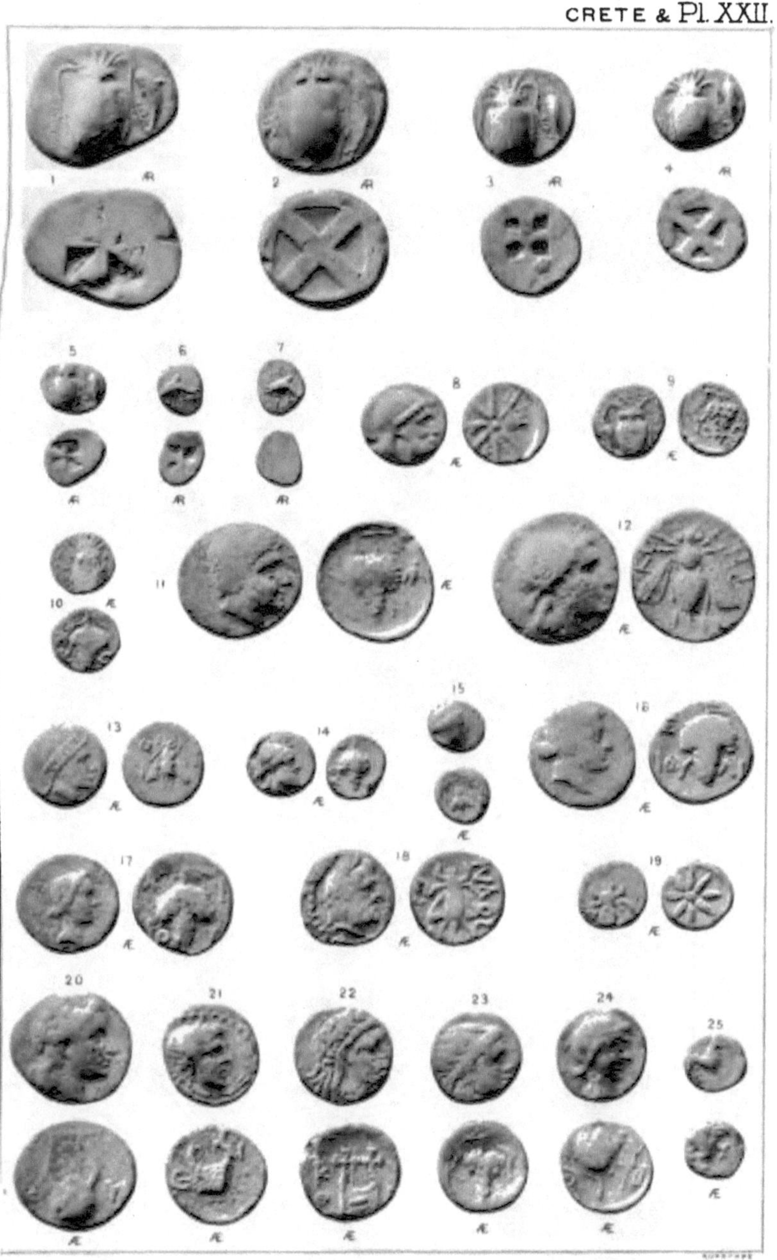

CEOS, CYTHNOS.

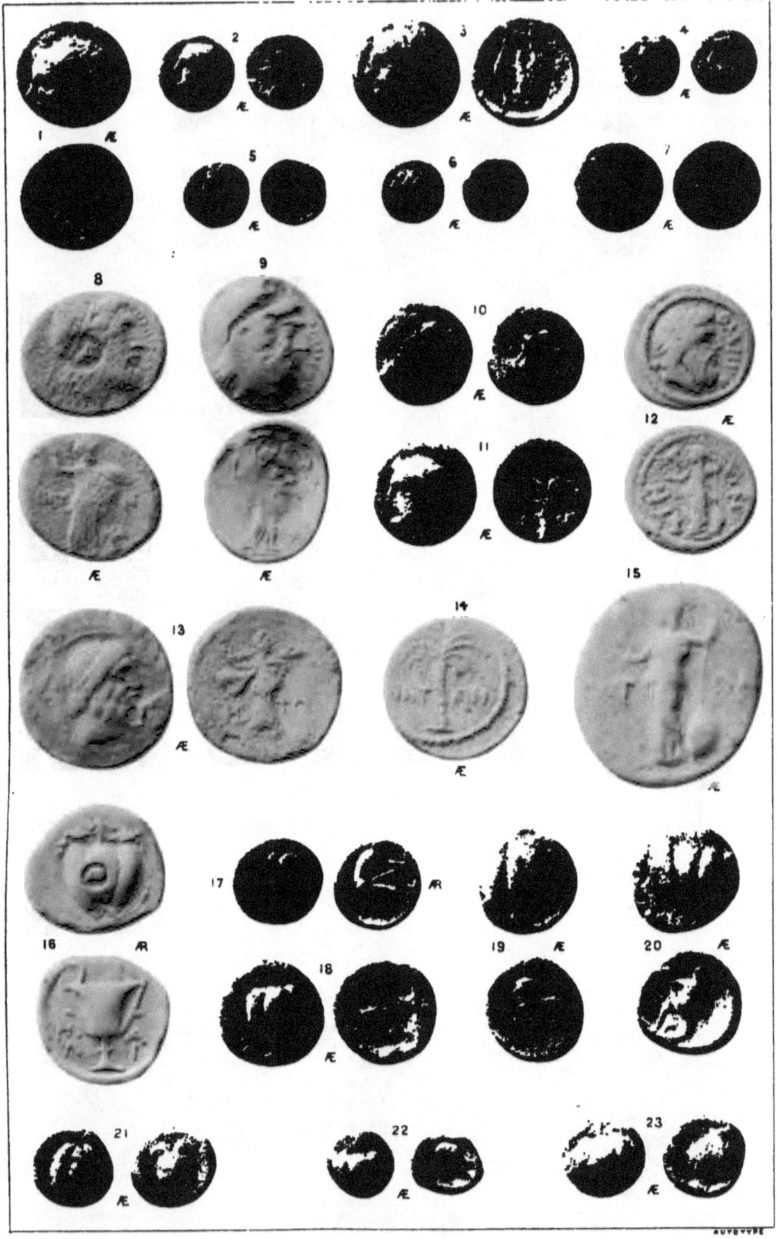

1 Æ 2 Æ 3 Æ 4 Æ 5 Æ 6 Æ 7 Æ 8 Æ 9 Æ 10 Æ 11 Æ 12 Æ 13 Æ 14 Æ 15 Æ 16 AR 17 AR 18 Æ 19 Æ 20 Æ 21 Æ 22 Æ 23 Æ

AUTOTYPE

DELOS—MELOS.

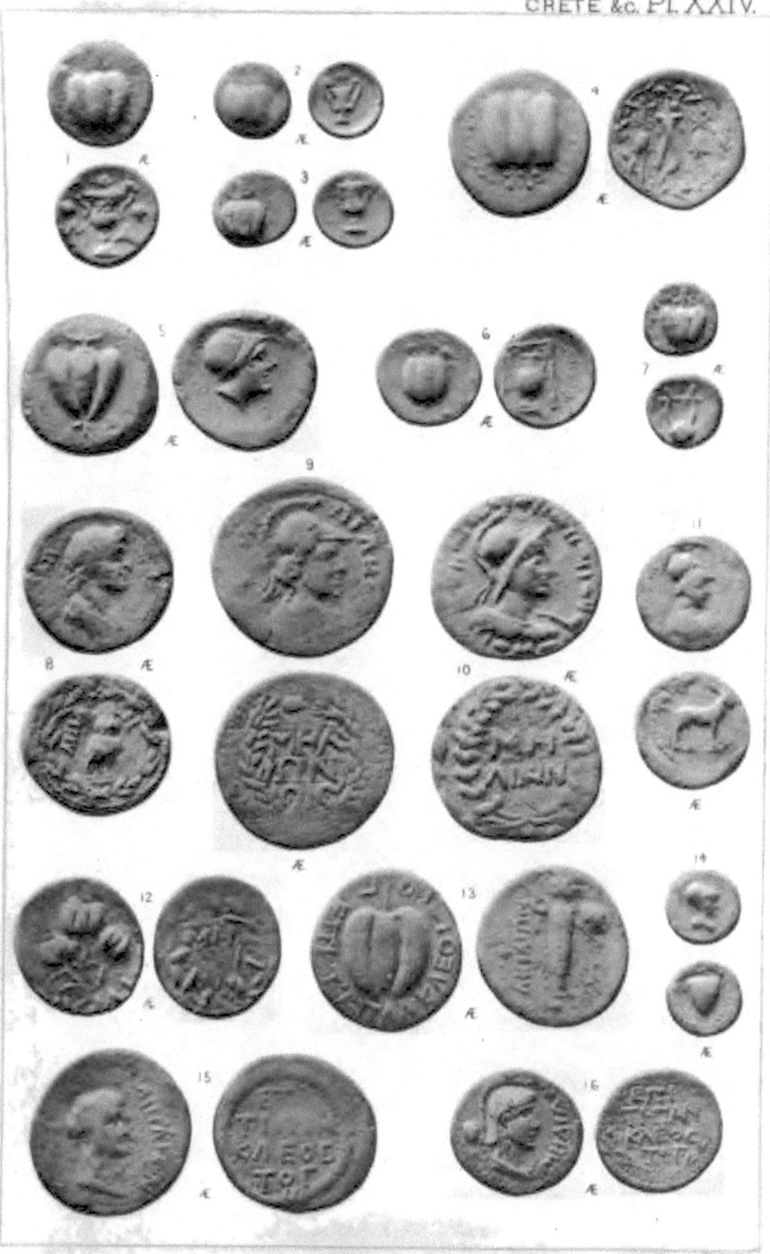

MELOS.

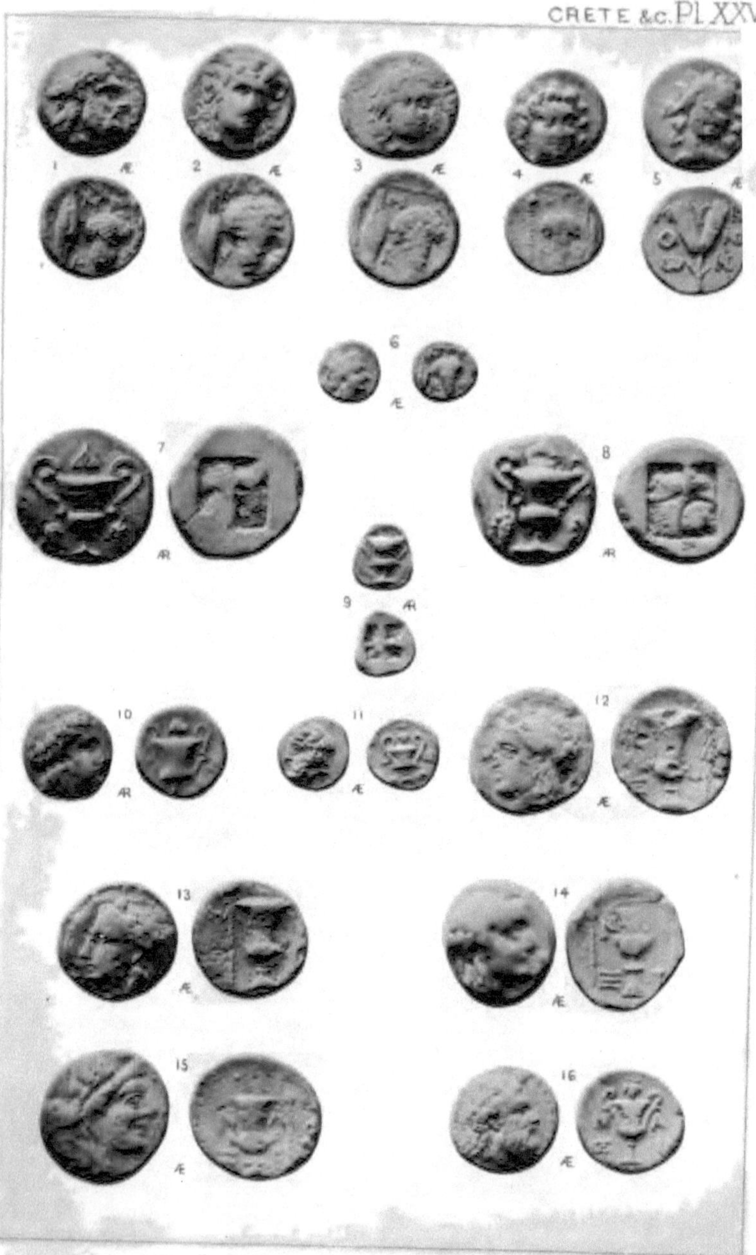

MYCONOS, NAXOS.

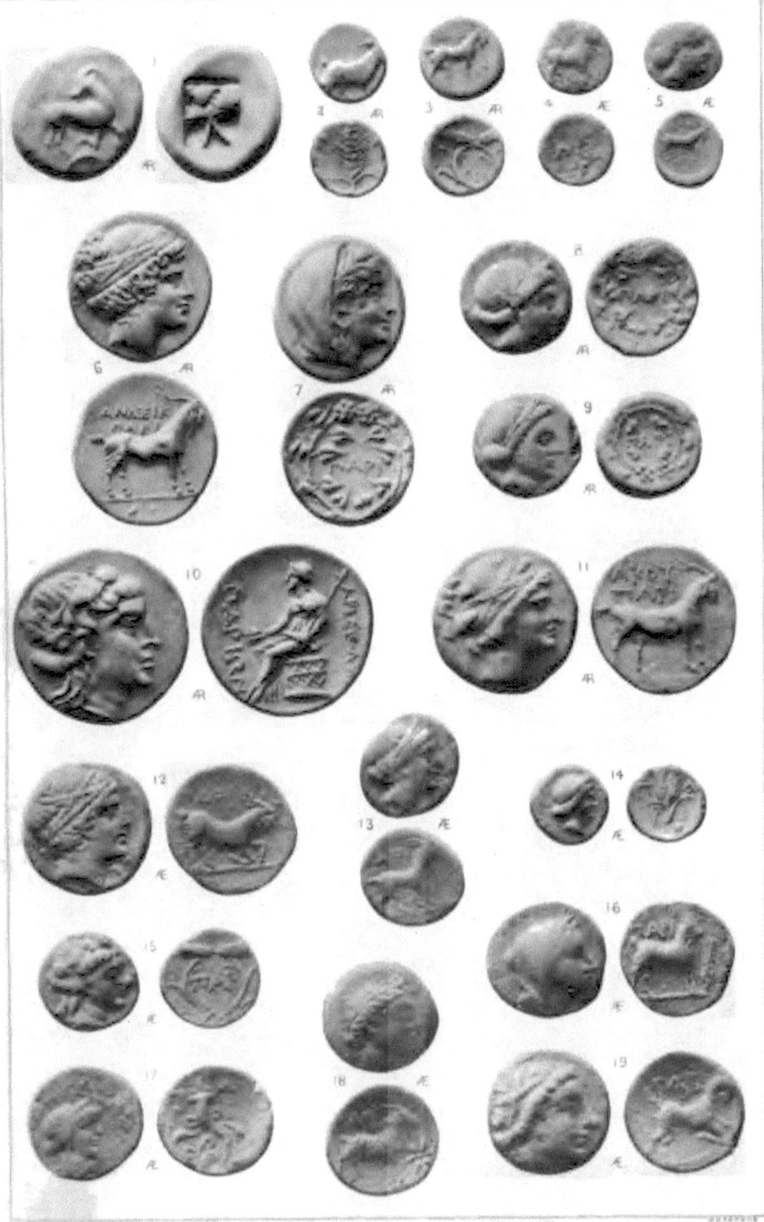

PAROS.

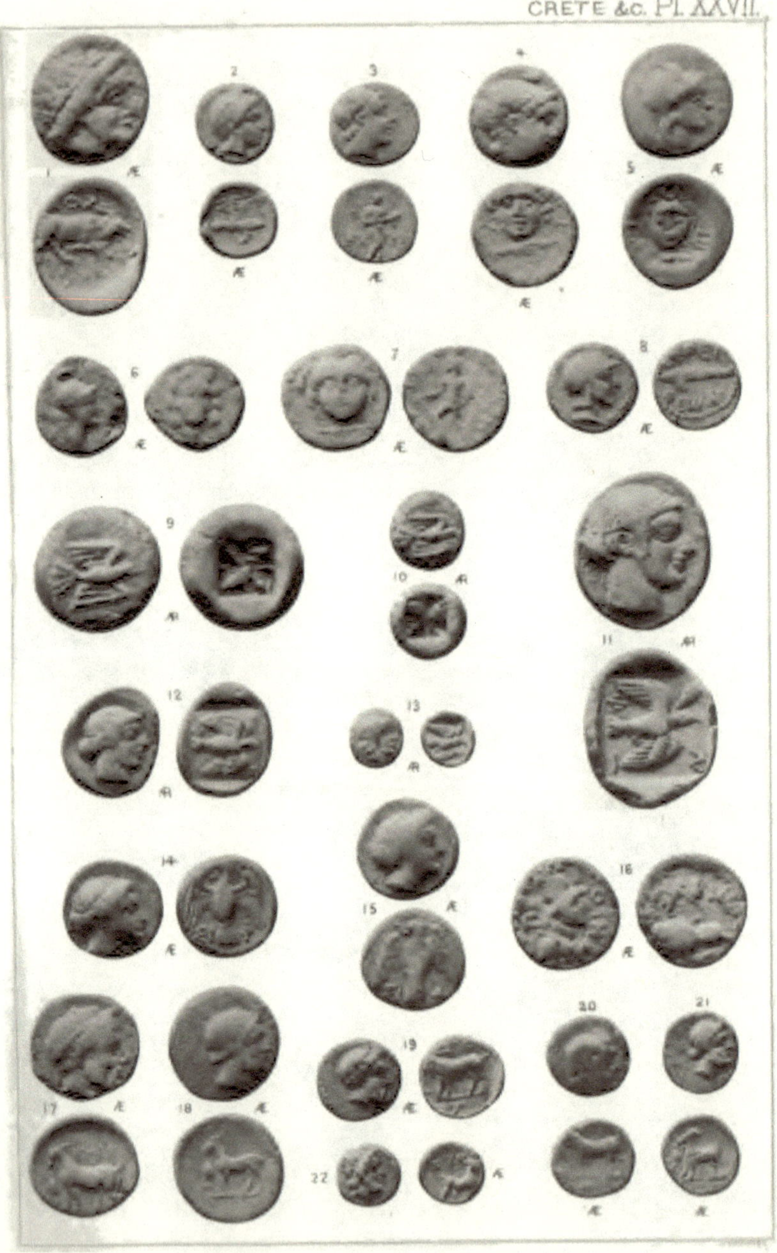

PHOLEGANDROS—SYROS.

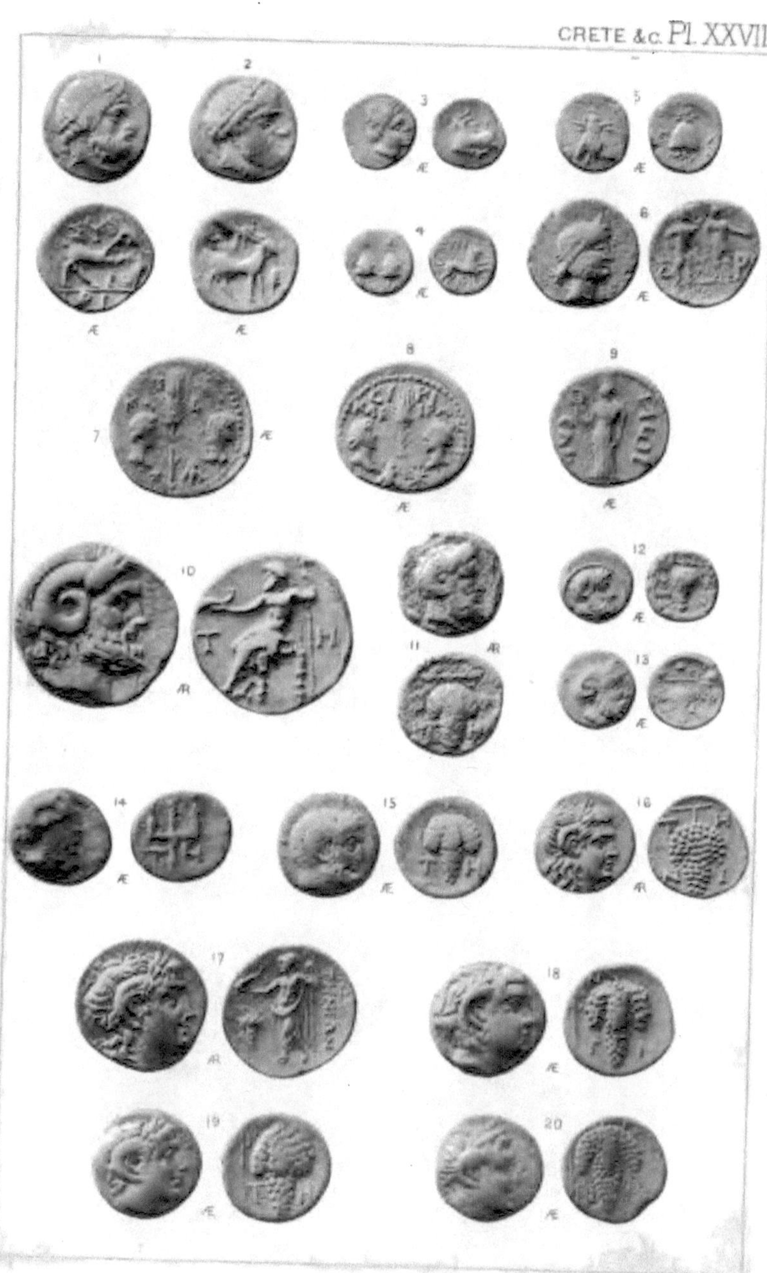

SYROS, TENOS.

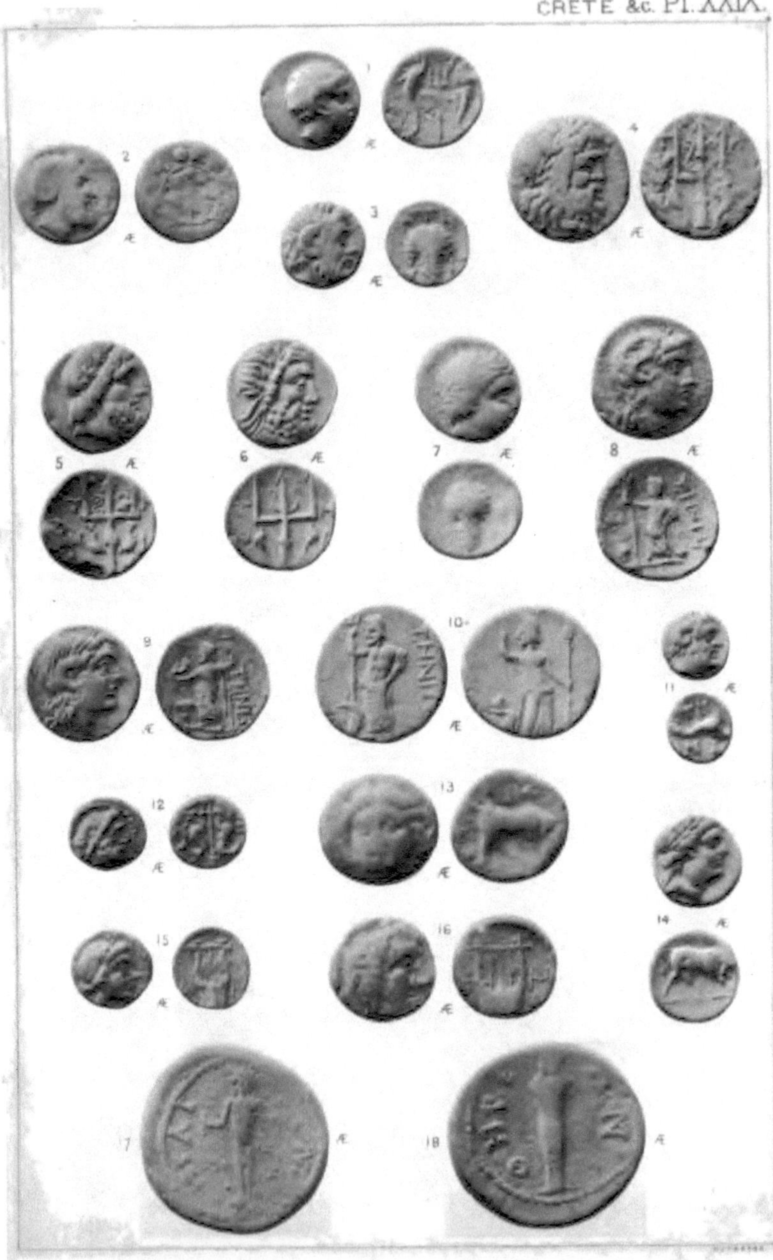

TENOS, THERA.

www.ingramcontent.com/pod-product-compliance
Lightning Source LLC
LaVergne TN
LVHW091132080826
845145LV00008B/2124

* 9 7 8 1 4 7 3 3 3 7 8 3 1 *